THE ANDEAN CODEX

Also by J. E. Williams
Viral Immunity
Prolonging Health

THE ANDEAN CODEX

ADVENTURES AND INITIATIONS
AMONG THE PERUVIAN SHAMANS

J.E. WILLIAMS

HAMPTON ROADS
PUBLISHING COMPANY, INC.

for the evolving human spirit

Hampton Roads Publishing Company, Inc.
1125 Stoney Ridge Road
Charlottesville, VA 22902

434-296-2772
fax: 434-296-5096
e-mail: hrpc@hrpub.com
www.hrpub.com

If you are unable to order this book from your local
bookseller, you may order directly from the publisher.
Call 1-800-766-8009, toll-free.

Library of Congress Cataloging-in-Publication Data

Williams, J. E. (James Eugene), 1949-
  The Andean codex : adventures and initiations among the Peruvian shamans/
J.E. Williams.
      p. cm.
  Summary: "A doctor recounts his travels with the shamans of the Peruvian
Q'ero tribe, including visits to the holy sites of Machu Picchu, Cuzco, and
Moray"--Provided by publisher.
  Includes bibliographical references.
  ISBN 1-57174-304-9 (5-1/2x8-1/2 tp : alk. paper)
  1. Quero Indians--Religion. 2. Quero Indians--Rites and ceremonies. 3.
Shamanism--Peru. 4. Ayahuasca ceremony--Peru. 5. Initiation rites--Peru.
6. Peru--Religious life and customs. 7. Peru--Social life and customs.
8. Williams, J. E. (James Eugene), 1949- I. Title.
  F3430.1.Q47W56 2005
  299.8'8323--dc22
                                    2005012723

ISBN 1-57174-304-9
10 9 8 7 6 5 4 3 2 1
Printed on acid-free paper in Canada

In Memory of Sister Thedra
(1900–1992)
and
Jorge Palqar Flores
(1978–2005)

Contents

Acknowledgments

This book is a product of many people. Thanks go to Gerald Hausman who coaxed it out of me, Bernard Gunther for his insights and suggestions, Melvis Lara who tolerated my long absences in Peru, and Frank DeMarco, my publisher at Hampton Roads, for believing in the book and for his patience over the many years it took me to write it.

My appreciation goes to the Villacorta-Chong family of Iquitos and Lima, particularly to Rosita Chong and her brother Roger, who graciously opened their homes to me and with whom I stay on all my trips to Peru. They made it possible for me to navigate Peruvian culture, introduced me to its cuisine and customs, provided endless connections and information, and helped in every way imaginable. Their generosity and friendship made every trip to Peru special and amiable.

In Cuzco, many provided invaluable introductions, insights, and encouragement. In particular, I thank Maria Antonieta Peña Garcia who helped at critical moments on my personal shamanic journey. Very special thanks to Jackeline Fernandez Baca Urruchi, her husband, Julio Camacho, and family of four generations with whom I stay in Cuzco. Thanks to Mayela Inya and Alfredo Delare; to Jesus Garcia Tapia of the Academia Mayor de la Lengua Quechua, who helped with my Quechua; and especially to Antón Ponce de León Paiva of Semana Wasi in Urubamba for helping me stay focused on the deeper spiritual issues of the Andean teachings.

From Lima, my appreciation goes to Maya Hein, her brother Mark, and Cesar Ravenna, who now lives in Los Angeles, for their insights into the Peruvian soul. Along the ayahuasca trail, many thanks to Ana Varela, Alan and Mariella Shoemaker, Scott Peterson of the Refugio Altiplano, the urban shamaness Blanca Pinto of Lima, and Elsa Rengifo of the Instituto para Investigaciónes Amazonias Peruanas. My deep gratitude goes to the Shipibo shamans Benjamin Mahua, Guillermo Arevalo, and Leoncio Garcia who cared for me with tenderness, guided me with the wisdom of true forest shamans, and guarded my inner journeys with their knowledge and strength.

I acknowledge those who have gone before me to Q'ero, especially the Peruvian anthropologist Oscar Nunez del Prado, his son Juan Nunez who carries on the family tradition, and Americo Yabar of Cuzco, Juan Ruiz from Mexico, and the Cuhan-American psychologist Alberto Villodo who helped initiate the paradigm for Andean spirituality.

Without the special connection and companionship of the Q'ero *pampamesayoq* Sebastian Palqar Flores, this book would not have been possible. My love extends to his brother, Jorge Palqar Flores, who died of an acute illness in March 2005, and to my god-families in the mountains of Q'ero.

Author's Note

The experiences in this book are true and took place as described. All of my work in Peru has been among Peruvians, both friends and researchers, and with Indians and shamans. None of the experiences recounted in this book are the result of participation with commercial tours. In fact, I have never been on one. Since I am fluent in Spanish and speak some Quechua, the transmission of knowledge has been direct. In all cases in this book, I have discussed my intent with my indigenous mentors and Peruvian friends and have received approval and permission to use material and photographs. A portion of the proceeds from sales of this book goes directly to the Q'ero.

For readability, I've used common words for plants and animals, and listed scientific names in the glossary rather than in the text. Bibliographic information is provided in a list of references rather than footnoted. Locations and physical places described in the text are geographically accurate, though in some instances I choose to remain vague and not provide detailed information because the areas in question are sacred places. Maps are also accurate but are simplified sketches representative of the areas described. They are meant to provide visual resonance with the text and not to serve as cartographical guides.

The range of Quechua spellings for the same or similar words is astonishing. For consistency, I've used *Diccionario Quechua* from the Academia Mayor de la Lengua Quechua as my source for Quechua terms. These are in italics and remain italicized throughout the text. Spanish words (unless in common English usage) are also italicized. Commonly used Quechua words for places like Cuzco and Pisac are not in italics. A glossary of Quechua and Spanish terms is provided at the end of the book.

A few words on why I chose to use the word "codex" in the title of this book: A codex refers to a manuscript of a classical work, particularly a religious or spiritual scripture. In Mesoamerica, central Mexico to southern Guatemala, a number of codices existed. Both the Aztec and Mayan cultures had a sophisticated form of pictographic written language and recorded their history, genealogies, astronomical charts, divinatory tables, calendars, religious ceremonies, medicinal plants, and deities in stone, on bark paper, or on deer hide.

During the conquest, Spanish priests burned countless numbers of codices. Those that survived were sent to Europe where some have been preserved and are now available as photographic facsimiles. Following the initial stages of the conquest, a few insightful priests recognized the importance of chronicling indigenous practices and beliefs. Collaborating with indigenous artists, several beautifully executed codices were reproduced in Spanish.

The Incas did not have a written language, so no pre-Hispanic codices were found in Peru. Unlike in Mexico, even in postconquest times, few written manuscripts on Peru are preserved. Therefore, I chose the word "codex" for the title because the time has come for a book representing Andean spiritual life that gives this tradition the respect it deserves. I do this by recounting my adventures with the Q'ero, distilling what I learned, and outlining the five ethical principles of the Andean way of life, as well as giving an overview of Incan cosmology and the initiations that occur along the path of the shaman.

Preface

The events in this book, my experiences with the Q'ero Indians, took place between 1996 and 2004 in an isolated part of the Peruvian Andes in a legendary land where a handful of shaman-priests are the custodians of an ancient knowledge of how the natural world operates. Bordered by snow-capped mountains on one side, it is accessible only by crossing passes at elevations up to 18,500 feet. On the other, it is protected by the remote Madre de Dios jungle and beyond that the immense Amazon rain forest of Brazil. Here members of the Q'ero Nation, a group of about one thousand individuals, divided between eight villages, carry on pastoral and agricultural practices much as their ancestors have done for thousands of years. This book summarizes the Andean teachings based on a way of life reaching back to a time before the Incas.

In order to survive the extremes of high-altitude living, the Q'ero not only need to be masters of their physical domain, but must also live a cooperative lifestyle in harmony with each other and their environment. This necessitates a worldview and way of life that encompass ethical and spiritual guidelines—the five principles of the Andean Codex—based on a mystical relationship with the Earth, which they call *Pachamama*. More than anything else, it is this mystical quality that characterizes the Q'ero, whose lifestyle embodies the teachings of the Andes.

The Q'ero taught me a new way to look at the world. In essence, it is composed of five fundamental principles, covered in detail in this book.

The first three principles are *munay, yachay,* and *llank'ay,* which form the core teachings of the Q'ero. Think of them as the ability to feel, to think, and to act. According to Andean belief, when our emotions, thoughts, and actions are aligned, we are balanced human beings. Balance promotes harmony. Health follows as a natural consequence. Then peace and happiness can exist.

Munay represents feelings and emotions, and means love and amiability. Its outer expression is natural beauty and loveliness. In its highest form, *munay* manifests through benevolence or lovingkindness and reflects the harmony of nature in one's character. *Yachay* means to learn and to know and, in its highest form, suggests the superior consciousness one arrives at through the proper cultivation of Andean principles. *Llank'ay* means to labor and suggests the attitude of service through physical work. In modern times, this may be interpreted to include mental and creative work. In its highest form, it manifests as personal power and physical strength achieved through self-discipline.

A fourth principle, *kawsay* or life, forms the matrix for the first three. In Andean tradition, all things in the natural world, animate or inanimate, are imbued with living energy. Andean cosmology informs us that all elements of the Earth are connected by a web of living energy, *kawsay pacha* in Quechua. Lightning, animals, trees, rocks, birds, insects, and rain compose and populate the Andean mystical landscape. The mountain peaks or *Apus* are temples. Coca leaves speak and stones heal. The purpose of human life is to achieve and maintain balance between the human sphere and nature. This is accomplished through attunement with the world of living energy. In this way, the continuity of life is assured not only for the individual but for the community and future generations; in our times, this includes the entire planet.

Ayni is the fifth principle. It emphasizes reciprocity and constitutes the central theme of the Andean way. It manifests as mutual sharing, respect, and understanding of the needs of others. Without reciprocity, there is no renewal cycle. By reciprocating all the good that comes to you from others, nature, and the spirit world, you become more benevolent. In doing so, the circle of life is complete.

Though Andean wisdom is timeless and arises from the same universal source of truth as all esoteric teachings found throughout the world's great cultures, there are two things unique about this teaching. One: it forms a continuous cultural thread extending from before the Incas to the present and is therefore unique in the Americas. Two: it contains a pragmatic ecospiritual healing message vital in our times of global environmental destruction and individual existential angst. In this sense, it is not a religion or philosophy, but a way of life that embodies ethical, moral, and spiritual guidelines.

The healing message as taught to me by the Q'ero and presented in this book is simple: Clear your heart; love deeply; harmonize your thoughts and feelings; align your efforts to do your best; and respect the natural environment.

J. E. Williams
Lima, Peru
2004

Ayahuasca Spirits

The ayahuasca shaman, or *ayahuascero,* Don Pedro is tall for a mestizo and as lean as a vine. This talkative man in his early sixties with deep-set obsidian eyes in a weathered-looking but kind face spends much of his time sitting and is in no hurry to start. Unaware of the heat, he passes time entertaining us with tales of his training with a female shaman in the jungles near Ecuador, an unusual apprenticeship as most Amazonian shamans are men. When his wife and children are asleep, he rises slowly from his stool, being careful not to hit his head on the low thatched ceiling, and leads us to the ceremonial hut behind his home, where he immediately settles into a straight-backed chair.

A human skull brown with age peers hollow-eyed from a wooden trunk. Beside the *ayahuascero* is a three-foot-long crocodile skull bleached by the sun. Directly behind him on a plain table stands an ornate silver crucifix. A slight breeze penetrates the thin reed walls and rattles the tin roof of the hut. The candles flicker and the crucifix and the skull do a shadow dance. In front of Don Pedro on another wooden table sits a bottle of a yellowish-brown liquid. Alongside it is a small cup. Otherwise the room is empty.

I sit on a bench cut from a log. It is hard and uncomfortable. Sweat pools in the hollows above my collarbone and drips down my chest. The Peruvian poet Ana Varela sits beside me. Her high-cheekboned face shines with sweat in the candlelight and there are beads of sweat along her neck.

By ten at night, the breeze, our only ally against the stifling Amazonian heat, has dissipated. Other than the sound of the tree frogs pulsing on and off, the silence is so thick it feels like cloth pressed against my skin.

"Tonight we drink *yajé*," the *ayahuascero* says, his voice resonant and serious. "Your mind may open and your heart sing. You may vomit violently. Don't be afraid. Prepare yourselves."

Like an early explorer about to embark on a journey to the New World, I am filled with a mixture of wonder and fear. I listen attentively, fascinated by everything Don Pedro says. I will discover later that I am naïve and unprepared for what I am about to experience.

I had read accounts of ayahuasca sessions by Westerners but found them limited in insight and lacking depth of experience. Accounts from the 1950s by anthropologists of ayahuasca visions recorded after sessions with Amazonian Indians were more dramatic, but academic. They told of visitations by supernatural beings, journeys with dolphins to cities under the Amazon River, and conversations with plant spirits. As a doctor, however, I hardly believed that an organic substance made from boiling the bark of a vine with some leaves that in themselves have limited chemical activity could produce the claimed effects. In less than an hour, I would find out how wrong my assumptions were.

Handing us plastic buckets in which to vomit, Don Pedro says, "*Yajé* is also called *la purga*."

He explains that, due to its potent emetic and laxative effects, ayahuasca cleanses the body, which accounts for the name, "the purge." *Yajé*, as mentioned, is another common way of referring to the ayahuasca brew. Shamans say that the vision-producing mixture of plants guides them in healing and facilitates attunement with the spirits of the forest.

Yajé expands the consciousness and integrates mind and body while harmonizing the individual with nature, so it is respectfully addressed as *Madre Ayahuasca.* In Peru, the most potent aspects of nature are believed to possess not only life but intelligence. In particular, plants such as corn, coca, tobacco, and ayahuasca have this active intelligence, and they are blessed by a *madre* or "mother" that makes them wise. The Earth Mother, *Pachamama,* is mother to them all. Peruvian shamans believe that plants not only nourish us and heal disease, but teach us about the environment and how to be a good-hearted and wise person. Such plant teachers are called *plantas maestras,* "master plants."

"Tomorrow morning, don't eat or drink anything before ten. Then drink one glass of warm lemon water with garlic. You can add a little salt. At noon, consume only chicken broth and eat nothing else for the rest of the afternoon," Don Pedro tells us, outlining the rules for after the ceremony. "In the evening, you can eat a meal, but don't add any salt, sugar, or oil. Don't eat fish or fruit."

Lighting *mapacho,* wild Amazonian tobacco commonly made into large hand-rolled cigarettes or used in small wooden pipes, the *ayahuascero* blows smoke over each of us and onto our palms. *Mapacho* belongs to the Solanaceae family of plants and is an extremely powerful intoxicant. When smoked in moderation, it can cause mild euphoria, muscle weakness, and stupor, then sleep (often with vivid dreams when smoked in excess). It is an integral part of Amazonian shamanic practice and is used extensively in healing ceremonies to cleanse the patient, much as North American Indians use the smoke from dried sage.

Don Pedro then pours a few drops of the pure cane alcohol called *aguardiente* on the dirt floor to honor *Pachamama.* Then he sprinkles some on each of the skulls to ignite the spirit within them. It is as if he is saying, "Drink with us, be alive tonight once again, protect and guide us in the world of the dead, in the worlds beyond what we see with our physical eyes."

In a barely audible voice, he invokes saints and forest spirits. Blowing smoke into the bottle of *yajé,* he covers it with his palm and softly whistles. The smoke trapped in the space between the top of the bottle and the yellowish-brown liquid swirls like eddies in a river. As he lifts his palm off the bottle some of the smoke escapes. As it drifts upward, the candlelight cuts through it and makes it look like lace. He blows into the bottle several times to awaken its energy by feeding its spirit with the life force contained in his breath.

Pouring some of the brew into a plastic cup, he drinks it in one swallow. Then he says, "Don't be afraid."

The smell is strong enough to turn one's stomach even before tasting it. Ana goes first. Her face twists as she drinks the thick substance. I hope that I will be able to swallow mine. She hands the cup back to Don Pedro and he fills it and gives it to me, watching intently as I bring it to my lips. The bitterness is not as strong as I expect. A foul aftertaste lingers on my tongue all the way to the back of my throat.

After I finish drinking, Don Pedro blows out the candles. Traditionally, ayahuasca ceremonies take place at night and in complete darkness. The heat is relentless and sweltering in the hut as we wait in the dark for the spirits to arrive. Don Pedro smokes another *mapacho* cigarette. The light from the match momentarily reveals his face and I see that his eyes are closed as if in contemplation. The smell is pungent but pleasant. Then, he whistles. The sound is soft and relaxing. After ten minutes, he chants the melodies called *icaros* considered by Amazonian shamans to be magical. They are said to be the songs the spirits of the plants sing. He accompanies himself with the rhythmical rustle of the *shacapa,* a simple form of musical device typical to ayahuasca ceremonies, made from the dried leaves of a low-growing palm in the Poaceae family.

Twenty minutes pass and I feel nothing except the oppressive heat. Then Ana moans.

"It's too strong," she says. *"Muy fuerte,"* she repeats several times in a trembling voice that sounds on the edge of hysteria.

I wonder if I am slow to react to its properties, or if Ana is exaggerating. When she retches violently and vomits into her plastic bucket, I know she is at least experiencing the purgative effects. She finishes vomiting and settles back on the bench beside me. I ask if she is all right. She tells me that the visions have started and then falls silent.

As an audience hushes and the orchestra becomes alert when the conductor comes on stage and taps his baton, so my brain stills and my body tenses. Though unaware of it at that moment, I am on the threshold of the experience that will shape the next decade of my life.

For the first few minutes, the experience is pleasurable, as when relaxing before sleep, but that rapidly progresses and I am propelled into the most extraordinarily beautiful and at times terrifying visionary world imaginable.

The room gives way and the walls disappear like a sand castle dissolves in the oncoming tide. It is as if all I am, and all that ever existed, is evaporating. I am frightened. This intense anxiety passes, however. Then, for a moment, I am floating in a void. Nothing exists except endless darkness. Suddenly, stars so bright they hurt my eyes appear. I recognize the Milky Way below me and a universe of stars all around. It is beautiful and grand and I don't feel alone or frightened. I am accompanied by light.

The dissolution of normal consciousness can be frightening. It is like death. It is not the end of the body, however, but of the multitude of opinions, thoughts, and memories that shape one's life. You are no longer what you thought you were and you are everything that you never would have imagined you could be. Amazonian shamans are said to die many times while alive. In doing so, they learn to let go of the mundane and to open themselves to the ancient teachings revealed in the forest and to the immensity of the universe. In Quechua, ayahuasca means "the vine of the dead."

In an instant, I descend toward Earth, free-falling, and the darkness fades. An orange sun rises in the distance and covers half the horizon. I float over the great Amazon rain forest, an endless sea of green extending to the horizon in four directions. Then I slowly fly east and head toward the rising sun. The river is like an immense brown serpent with watery tentacles that reach into the forest in every direction. As I float over it, the river seems less a waterway than a force of life. Animate and real, it pulses and writhes underneath me.

As I fly, the river changes. It becomes a monstrous ana-conda rising up from the water. Then the frightening snake opens its gargantuan mouth as if to devour me. Terrified for a moment, I overcome my fear as I realize that what is happening is inevitable. I think of Jonah and the whale. Instead of swallowing me, however, the snake lowers itself to the bank of the river and out of its mouth comes every kind of jungle animal, bird, and insect as if from Noah's Ark.

Later, I learn that a cosmic anaconda is central to Amazonian creation myths. The Amazon River is considered the mother of all life and the anaconda its representation. Giant anacondas, some over 40 feet long, are revered by the Indians. The ancestor of them all is called *Yakumama*. Legend has it that this snake is so huge it hasn't moved for ages and that trees grow from its back. Since snakes are the animals closest to the ground, they are thought to harbor the wisdom of the Earth.

The forest, *sach'a*, absorbs each creature as a sponge takes up drops of water. Then, as I watch, the giant anaconda dissolves into tens of thousands of smaller snakes. Many enter the forest as the animals did, while the rest slither into the river.

In the next instant, I am in the forest standing in the center of a circular clearing with trees all around. At first I am alone. Then every kind of forest animal appears. Some emerge from the shadows under the foliage. Others move in the trees bending branches and rustling leaves.

I call to them: *"Hermanitos,"* I say over and over again. "Little brothers."

Out of the forest they come. All types of jungle birds sit on my head and shoulders. Squirrels and monkeys cling to my arms and legs. Deer and tapir sit at my feet and snakes coil around my legs. Tears flow down my checks and my heart opens. I feel at one with the forest, the creatures in it, and the ancient spirits that empower it with life and energy.

The trees shimmer with lines of light like filaments that connect each leaf to the other. Then the trees disappear, leaving only myriad luminous fibers. At first, they appear random, ever changing, and in constant motion. Then I realize they pulse rhythmically and are arranged in geometric patterns.

In later work with the Shipibo Indians of the Ucayali River, I find that these patterns are typical during ayahuasca ceremonies. They are the fabric from which a shaman weaves healing spells. Like notes on a musical score, the shaman reads these patterns and sings the songs of the forest plants to cure the patient.

Then the original luminosity changes to a dazzling phosphorescent blue so beautiful it is painful to watch.

I repeat aloud, "It's too beautiful."

"Estás bien?" the *ayahuascero* asks.

"Si, estoy bien," I answer. "I'm all right, but it's so beautiful it hurts. Can you make it stop?"

"No, hijo," he says. "I can't, son. You are seeing reality now."

My brain is overwhelmed. I had read enough of the chemistry

of ayahuasca to know that it can modulate the same neurotransmitter, serotonin, influenced by certain antidepressants and drugs like 3,4-methylenedioxymethamphetamine (MDMA), popularly known as Ecstasy. If too much serotonin is released, it can cause dehydration and elevated blood pressure. Uncomfortable, I check the time on my watch and count my heart rate. It is just after midnight and my pulse is normal. Huge drops of sweat roll off my body. I feel feverish.

Don Pedro dips cold water from a bucket and pours it over me. Rivulets of water run down my neck and shoulders and onto the dirt floor. The water cools me and I begin to feel better.

Ana has long since fallen into a deep trance. The next day, she tells me that she had a long discussion with her deceased mother and, afterward, felt closure with her on many unresolved issues. At the moment, she lies stretched out on the bench as if dead.

The intense heat of earlier has passed, but the air is still and humid. The darkness is profound. I continue to see webs of geometric shapes, though not as bright as before. They seem alive and possessed of a kind of intelligence much like a neural network.

As when the conductor silences an orchestra between the different parts of a composition, there is a lull in the visions. My rational mind, unequipped for what is to come, has no basis with which to anchor itself and my intellect, normally my strongest attribute, is as useless as would be the paper on which my doctoral degree is printed in a deluge.

The *ayahuascero,* who has returned to his chair and has been softly chanting *icaros* and fanning Ana with the *shacapa,* stops. After several minutes of silence he says, "The spirits have arrived. Listen."

I am not sure what he means, but as I listen, I hear footsteps circling the hut so faint as to be barely audible.

"Tigre," he says.

A jaguar prowls the perimeter of the hut. It circles as jaguars do, closing ever so imperceptibly the distance between the prey and itself. Then it stops behind me. Stillness pervades the hut. So much time passes without a sound that I wonder if what I heard is real or my imagination.

In contrast to my thoughts, my body reacts automatically. The hairs on the back of my neck and arms stand up, my muscles tense, and I become acutely alert. I had a similar experience with a jaguar once before while conducting research on the Osa Peninsula of Costa Rica in 1969. In the morning, I found tracks circling my camp. They were so large that when I put my hand in them my fingertips didn't touch the edges.

Then it leaps.

Instead of landing heavily on my back as I expect, its body fluidly merges with mine. My hands become its paws and my neck its powerful muscular neck. Then the jaguar—me—running on all fours at an incredible speed, leaps over a precipice and enters a strange new world.

No longer in the forest, I am in a yellow desert landscape. Orange stones litter the terrain that spreads endlessly out before me. The jaguar's powerful body takes me farther into this magical place as I struggle to hold on to the memory of human form.

Losing normal consciousness and physical form by shapeshifting into the jaguar's body is frightening. It is as if I have ceased to exist and the universe I know and am comfortable in never existed. Though fragments of my consciousness remain, my ability to think dissolves like a film running in reverse. It takes me at lightning speed toward my own birth, into the womb, and beyond to a place before my grandparents were born. Among my last thoughts is that this is an ancient shamanic place, the parallel universe Indians talk about, a separate reality on the other side of normal human consciousness.

I can't calculate how far I travel in that land, but I sense that wherever I am going will soon be too far. I am afraid that if I continue, every fragment of my human consciousness will no longer exist and I may not be able to return. This is an unbearable thought and I am overcome with dread. But my initial fear diminishes quickly when I realize I have a choice. I can continue or go back. The decision is mine. To go on means to see what exists in the unknown territory and to go back is to regain my normal state of consciousness. I choose to return.

After this, the visions become less intense and fade like images dissolving on a computer screen. At the edge of the darkness, I see Indian women and children, naked, sitting in the forest and watching. I feel they have been there the entire time. Later, I learn from the Shipibo Indians that the spirits of their ancestors commonly observe the shaman during ayahuasca ceremonies.

No longer in the jaguar's body nor in the yellow and orange desert, but back again in the *ayahuascero*'s hut, I gradually begin to feel connected to my body. To prove to myself that I am whole, I touch my arms and legs and feel my forehead for signs of fever. My rational mind tells me that I might have been delirious. My temperature feels normal.

It's just before dawn and the coolness of early morning has replaced the horrific heat of the night. I am comfortable. Ana stirs and Don Pedro speaks to her. I need to be alone with my thoughts, and though my legs are unsteady, I walk outside and sit on a small stool.

The effects have worn off and I am cognizant again. Then I experience something that rocks my world.

A man of about 35 years old, meticulously dressed in a fashionable gray suit and tie, appears. It is my father. Though he died when I was still an infant, I recognize him from the memory of photographs my mother kept. We have the father-son conversation we never had, and he talks of his life before dying and how he has watched over me. I am deeply touched. Love pervades me. I smell orchids. He tells me that it is time I walk my life path without him. He smiles and gradually his image fades in the first light of dawn.

Don Pedro lights the candles. The light is inviting and I return to the hut. He appears shaken.

He petitions the ayahuasca spirit in a soft voice, repeating over and over again: "*Porqué, Madre,* why did you come so powerfully? *Porqué?*"

"In all my years of working with ayahuasca in over three hundred ceremonies," he tells me, "I have never experienced a session as intense with anyone on their first time. She has chosen you. That's clear. But I am not the one to teach you. It is too powerful and beyond my experience."

We go outside the hut into the early morning darkness. I am still slightly dizzy and my legs are weak, but my mind is clear.

"Walk around," he says and we continue to talk as we walk in the first light of morning.

"Go to the Andes to learn from the shamans in the high mountains. The mountain spirits are very powerful and will strengthen and prepare you. When you are ready, return to the forest and learn from *Madre Ayahuasca.* She will teach you directly all that you need to know about shamanism and your own life."

"Maestro, if I go to the Andes, how will I find these shamans and know when I am ready to return?"

"They will find you and you will know when it is time."

Synchronicity in the Andes

It is said that when the student is ready the master appears. In my case, nature was the master. Specifically, my teachers were *sach'amama,* the giant trees of the Amazon rain forests, and *Apus,* the mountain spirits of the Andes. It took me the greater part of my adult life to be ready, however. When I was, I found that the teaching, ancient beyond belief, was right in front of me. It only required a code to access it.

Like a living book, once I comprehended the principles behind what my physical senses revealed, I discovered the ways of the shamans. What was once a process so mysterious as to be incomprehensible became understandable. In time, I found that a profound, intelligent, and compassionate ordering principle exists just beneath the surface of normal consciousness. One of the ways it reveals itself is through synchronistic events.

Most people experience synchronicity from time to time, but they think it is only "coincidence." Synchronicity is when two simultaneously occurring events converge that appear to have no causal connection but meaning nevertheless exists between them. Such events provide the clues, if we are aware enough to recognize them and know how to read them, for making a connection between the universal organizing principle and our destiny. This implies that there is an interconnection between all things, including the events in a person's life. That interconnectedness can be thought of as the energetic matrix that holds life together.

I was soon to learn that on the shamanic path synchronicity occurs routinely and can reach an astonishing level. The adept shaman knows to step out of the way and let the natural order of things unfold. Along the way it helps to know how to read the clues nature provides. Peruvian shamans are experts in reading these patterns in nature. They use coca leaves or ayahuasca or other entheogenic substances for divination and as allies to help them understand the inner workings of nature and life. When such events occur regularly, they go beyond synchronicity to what I call shamanic resonance.

In October 2000, I return to Peru. Once there, Machu Picchu seems the obvious place to start. Unbeknownst to me, synchronicity is at work. I arrive in Cuzco just in time for a meeting about which I have no previous knowledge. Maria Antonieta, a Peruvian anthropologist, has organized a meeting between three Tibetan monks and three shamans from Q'ero. Having traveled from India to Europe, the monks are making their way across South America conducting ceremonies for world peace. The shamans, whom Maria has been closely involved with for years, have made the journey of several days out of the high mountains to Cuzco. While visiting one of the cathedrals, I see a flier about a Tibetan ceremony and phone for information. I attend and Maria and I have an immediate rapport. Though we only have time to talk briefly—I am later to learn that she is a person who speaks her mind without wasting time when necessary—she invites me to participate in a ceremony at Machu Picchu.

On the day of the event, I arrive at Aguas Calientes separately from the monks and shamans. By late morning, the monks in purple robes arrive with an international group of eight from Spain, Mexico, and Peru, all students of Buddhism who have sponsored the Tibetans' tour. The shamans wearing alpaca ponchos and knitted caps are shy and serious. The monks are also shy, but in contrast to the Q'ero, who are reserved, the Tibetans smile and talk easily. They speak no Spanish, however. As I am the only bilingual Spanish and English speaker, I become the translator. One monk speaks English and, after I translate from Spanish, he translates what I say into Tibetan for the other monks. Maria translates from Spanish to Quechua for the shamans.

Andean ceremonies traditionally take place at noon. We climb to a spot high above the ruins and wait for the sun to reach its zenith. The morning clouds and mist have disappeared and the sun warms us from a blue sky. When the sun is directly overhead, the Q'ero shamans invoke the spirits of Machu Picchu and the surrounding *Apus* by offering coca leaves. The Tibetans chant in deep bass voices and blow long ceremonial horns. We all share coca leaves. I am enthralled.

After the ceremony, the group, anxious not to miss the train back to Cuzco, quickly disperses. The Q'ero seem to vanish. I am left with the Tibetans. Standing at a prominent point overlooking the ruins, the river below and mountains to the east, I discuss Buddhist philosophy with the monk who speaks English. He is unusually tall. We talk of the changes in the world, the dilution of the Dharma during the modern era, and the last years of the Buddha when he stopped teaching and only prophesied. But it isn't long before the natural beauty eclipses our philosophical discussion and we are silent.

As we stand together overlooking the ruins, the tall monk tells me that, though he was born in Tibet, raised in Nepal, and lived in northern India in the shadows of the Himalayas, he has never seen anything like Machu Picchu.

"This may be the most beautiful place on Earth," he says with the utmost sincerity.

I agree. No matter how many times one visits Machu Picchu, it is as magical and beautiful as the first time, perhaps more so.

In Quechua, *picchu* means a pyramid-shaped mountain and *machu* signifies ancient or venerable, therefore the literal translation of Machu Picchu is "old mountain." In Quechua, words can have multiple meanings; therefore, a better interpretation is "sovereign guardian spirit of peace," which is why Machu Picchu has been called the City of Hope, the Crystal City, the City of Light, the Sacred City, and the City of Peace.

The least spoiled of South America's ancient ruins, the rocks and stones here, sacred to the Incas, remain undamaged except for the minimal effects of erosion from wind and rain. At an elevation of 8,040 feet (3,000 feet lower than Cuzco) with a drop of several thousand feet to the Urubamba River below, Machu Picchu is among the world's most visited archeological sites. Here, many of the natural elements crucial to Incan cosmology converge. Mountains, rocks, sun, water, moon, rainbows, the Earth, and Incan stonework form a unified esthetic whole.

Religious ceremonies and spiritual initiations have occurred and still take place here. Due to the extensive number of shrines and carved stones found here, which are used to observe the passage of the sun, it has served as a powerful ritual center. Machu Picchu's primary purpose, however, was as a sanctuary for *akllas* ("divine virgins of the sun") and *mamakunas* ("wise women"). It was the residence of the most powerful *layqas* ("female sorcerers and healers") in the Incan empire.

Set like a jewel atop a mountain in the midst of even higher green peaks, Machu Picchu is one part of a pair (*yanantin* in Quechua) of mountains, the other being Wayna Picchu. Respectfully referred to as Apu Machu Picchu by Andean shamans, the mountain complex also includes Apu Putukusi, a smaller, rounder peak east of Machu Picchu considered the guardian spirit of the area.

Surrounding Apu Putukusi is a ring of other mountains, and over the river to the west rise Machu Picchu and Wayna Picchu. Behind them is Inti Pata. Directly behind Putukusi to the east is Sachapata, and forming a semicircle around them are San Miguel, San Gabriel, and other mountains.

A valley with a year-round temperate climate lies between the mountains, and the Urubamba River runs through it. In Incan times, it was called the *Willkamayu* or Sacred River, considered the earthly reflection of *Mayu,* the river of stars that compose the Milky Way.

The theme of stellar phenomena mirrored on Earth, particularly the Milky Way, repeats like the melody of a musical composition in the Incan cosmic vision. As the basis of Andean astronomical observation and cosmological belief, the relationship of heavenly phenomena and events mirrored on Earth served as a ritual axis for the Incas.

The Sacred Valley of the Incas begins in Pisac, a town about 20 miles northeast of Cuzco. The river and the valley it creates wind south for about 60 miles toward Ollantaytambo. Beyond that is Machu Picchu. The Cordillera Vilcanota or Urubamba Mountains, a snowcapped mountain chain composed of numerous sacred peaks, forms the eastern border of the valley. To the west is a steep canyon wall topped with rolling plains planted with potatoes and Andean corn.

The Urubamba River, its water the color of the sky where it emerges from the Andes, slows as it reaches Machu Picchu. There it flows in semicircles around the mountains and changes color to an earthen brown. Beyond Machu Picchu, it enters the jungle and far beyond that it merges with the Ucayali River. Eventually, it becomes the turbulent upper Amazon before it is lost in the deep waters of that great river.

The cloud forests begin at Machu Picchu. Moisture and heat rise from the jungle and cause it to be frequently wrapped in thick fog and drenched from mist. The biodiversity of the area, a national preserve called the Historical Sanctuary of Machu Picchu, is rich in animals and plants. There are more than 50 species of mammals, including the rare short-faced Andean spectacled bear, and more than 60 species of reptiles, amphibians, and fish. The species of insects are uncountable, including more than seven hundred types of butterflies. Birds are especially plentiful with more than four hundred species, including toucans, wild pigeons, parakeets, hummingbirds, and quetzals. More than three thousand kinds of flowering plants, including orchids, begonias, and fuschias, have been counted in the sanctuary.

The Tibetans and their sponsors have left to catch the train back to Cuzco. The Q'ero have disappeared into the mist. Clouds rise from the river and flow along the mountain valleys like white streams transforming the landscape into a place of supernatural beauty. Row upon row of mountains spreads out before me to the east. Late afternoon sunlight filters through the mist and, shining from behind the mountains, fractures into hundreds of luminescent rays. I alone remain among the stones of Machu Picchu.

Standing on a rock ledge as I watch the changing scenery, my emotions, conflicted in the previous months, settle so deeply it feels like being in love.

Then I make my way down the mountain to Aguas Calientes, a charming place with a wonderful temperate climate surrounded by majestic cliffs. Once a simple village and a quick train stop on the way to Quillabamba, the former last stop on the train line until a massive landslide tore out an entire hillside from under the tracks, Aguas Calientes was never completely rebuilt; it is now a haphazard collection of structures at the end of the line. The current tourist train, an efficient European-style system, runs several times a day from Cuzco. A local train also operates on the same track, but in contrast to the tourist train, it is notoriously unreliable and always overcrowded.

I purchased the only passage available on the day of the ceremony, a one-way ticket, so now I have to find another to return. At the ticket counter, the clerk informs me that there are no tickets available on either of the two tourist trains. Seats are booked a week ahead, but he offers an alternative. If I go to where the passengers board, I might be lucky to get standing space on the local train. Of course, this means buying passage directly from the conductor and at a premium.

Heading in the direction he points, I walk along a cement causeway next to the tracks. After passing a collage of shops, I come upon a crowd of at least four hundred anxious and tired people, all with the same goal as mine. After speaking with a few, I find that some have been waiting for days. To add to the tension, the train is two hours late and these people are becoming more impatient by the minute. A few are hostile and jostle their way to stay in front of the swelling mass of backpackers, Andean farmers, and Indians. Getting out of Aguas Calientes today seems hopeless.

Turning away from the crowd, I make my way back with the idea of finding a hotel for the night. Not more than ten steps away, however, I see the three Q'ero sitting on the ground, their ponchos wrapped around them.

Surprised to see them and hopeful that we might have a conversation, I go up to them and ask: "Do you speak Spanish?"

"A little," one of the men responds. He gestures toward the oldest of the three. "He doesn't speak or understand any."

The older man, who speaks only Quechua, appears to be in his seventies. He pays no attention to what we are saying and looks off as if seeing something in the distance. He has an otherworldly look as if the events going on around him are so mundane they are unworthy of his attention. The youngest of the three looks at me as if he also doesn't speak Spanish, or is too shy to say that he does.

All three wear rubber sandals. Their ponchos are gray and

brown, but their knitted caps are bright yellow, orange, blue, and red. They remember me from the ceremony and seem interested in conversation.

"Have you eaten?" I ask.

They haven't, and I invite them into a small restaurant where I order us a meal. While we eat, they don't speak. When we finish, they thank me profusely in Quechua and we walk back to the station to check on the status of the train.

I had read of the Q'ero before coming to Peru. They are legendary throughout the Andes. Considered to have maintained the purest form of an ancient way extending back to a time before the Incas, they are thought to have among them the most traditional and powerful shamans. Conservative, reclusive, closed to outsiders, reluctant to relate even to Peruvians, the Q'ero have the reputation of being unapproachable. Yet, here I am standing alongside three Q'ero shamans who had performed the ceremony on Machu Picchu. How improbable to meet them when only a few days before I had been in California and had arrived in Cuzco without knowing a single person.

We stand and survey the crowd. We don't talk, but they exchange a word or two in Quechua.

Finally, the one who speaks some Spanish asks, "What do they call you?"

"Santiago," I answer, telling him the name I was given many years before in Mexico where I apprenticed with *curanderos* to study healing plants. "And your name?"

"I am Sebastian. This is my brother Jorge." He doesn't give me the older man's name.

After what seems like hours, the train rolls into the station. Well before it comes to a complete stop, the crowd swells off the platform and onto the tracks. Blue-jacketed conductors warn them back, yelling through bullhorns that they will let us know when it is time to board. Only passengers holding valid tickets are allowed closer to the train, where the conductors inspect the tickets, scrutinizing each one several times before handing it back to the passenger. Through the soot-coated windows, I see the train is already full and wonder how more passengers even with valid tickets can fit in.

An hour and a half passes. Meanwhile, the conductors continue checking tickets and board more passengers. Unexpectedly, the train lurches and some people lose their balance and fall onto others. Some think the train is about to pull away from the station and panic. They try to force their way into any last available space even if standing room only. The cars buck again, and the sound of metal against metal echoes off the surrounding mountain walls. A conductor yells the last call above the noise of the crowd and says that anyone with a confirmed ticket must come forward.

The Q'ero stand passively and watch from behind the crowd. I, on the other hand, am anxious to leave but don't have a ticket. I hope against the odds that an empty seat will turn up at the last minute. But the wall of people in front of us suggests that I will have to wait until tomorrow.

"Don't you have tickets?" I am unable to believe that the shamans would be invited to conduct ceremonies and not be given a return passage.

"No," Sebastian said. He stands complacently as if it matters little if he gets on the last train of the day, or tomorrow, or even the day after.

I ask again, "Are you sure you don't have a ticket?"

He replies as before, "No."

"Did they give you a piece of paper?" I try another line of reasoning.

"Yes," Sebastian says. "They gave us some slips of paper, but we don't know what they're for."

Realizing that Sebastian can't read Spanish, I ask to see the papers. He opens the cloth bundle that he carries on his back and hands me three return tickets to Cuzco.

"Where will you sit, Santiago?" he asks.

"I don't have a ticket. I'll have to go tomorrow or the next day." I reassure him that everything is okay and they should get on the train.

In truth, I have no idea when I'll get out, or if I'll ever see them again.

There is no time for talk. The train is leaving. It lurches forward and the iron wheels grate on the rusty tracks. Holding the three tickets over my head I shout to the conductor of the last car and push my way through the crowd with Sebastian, Jorge, and the third Q'ero behind me. The conductor waves us on, but when he sees the Indians, his expression is of disdain. He might as well have shouted that all Indians can wait. I insist that they have valid tickets with seat assignments, and he relents.

The train is already filled to capacity, but the crowd continues to push forward, forcing the conductor against the car railing. He orders them back. I shove Sebastian and the other Q'ero from behind, squeezing them into the already overcrowded car. There is no time for good-byes or to make arrangements to meet later, as they are swallowed up in the turmoil.

Then at the last moment, just as the train is pulling away, a conductor several cars ahead of where the Q'ero are waves me on. Without hesitating, I push my way through the throng and climb on board just as the train pulls out of the station. The conductor says, "You can ride as far as Ollantaytambo. We have ticketed passengers getting on there. You can get a bus to Cuzco tomorrow morning."

The next morning, walking in the center of Cuzco, I encounter Sebastian and Jorge sitting on a bench in the Plaza de Armas. They are on their feet before I reach them and greet me as if I were a distinguished but forgetful professor late for an appointment.

"Santiago, we've been waiting for you," Sebastian says.

Jorge smiles shyly and nods in agreement. The third Q'ero is absent. I am not to see him again for several years. Jorge, I am to discover, speaks a passable Spanish but is too reserved to speak directly to me.

"*Vamos*," Sebastian says. "Let's go."

Without wasting time or waiting for me to reply, they pick up their bundles, sling them over their backs, and tie them securely in front with a knot. I follow them to a small café on a side street several blocks from the plaza.

Over the next six years, this way of meeting will be the norm between us. Though they come to Cuzco infrequently, my once or twice a year arrivals manage to coincide with theirs. At first, I found this difficult to comprehend. Later, I am to learn that there are no coincidences. Though there are no phones within several days' walk of where the Q'ero live, either on the day I arrive or at the latest the following morning, Sebastian, sometimes alone and at other times with Jorge, arrives to welcome me back. These inexplicable meetings occur on every visit. Now, four years later, I am accustomed to the synchronicity.

Ruins of Machu Picchu with Wayna Picchu in the background

Light around Wayna Picchu

Wayna Picchu covered in clouds

Incan carved stone concealing a royal burial site

Intiwatana or the solar watch stone with three steps representative of the three worlds of Incan cosmology

Author, Sebastian, and Tibetan monk. Wayna Picchu in the background

The Shaman's Shadow

In this way, I began my relationship with the shaman-priest Sebastian Palqar Flores and my apprenticeship in Andean shamanism. Not only has he been ever since my primary mentor in studying Q'ero shamanic practices, but also my friend.

Q'ero shaman-priests are called *paqos*, specialists in ritual worship and communication with *Pachamama*, the *Awkikuna*, and the *Apus*. These are Quechua words that signify the spirit of the Earth, nature spirits, and the mountain spirits.

Though Sebastian is also a well-known *curandero* who practices divination with coca leaves, for which his services are in demand when he visits Cuzco, there is nothing pretentious about him. Forty-four years old, he is as rugged as the land from which he comes. He wears the pre-Hispanic black tunic or *unku* under a handwoven beige poncho of alpaca wool with thin brightly colored stripes near the borders, the trademark style of the Q'ero. When performing ceremonies, he changes his plain poncho for a multicolored one displaying geometric designs symbolic of the sun, moon, lakes, and stars. Over close-cropped black hair, he wears the traditional knitted Incan cap, the *ch'ullu*, which frames his sun-darkened face. He never wears shoes, preferring Andean sandals, which he wears to walk over jagged stones, through glacial streams, and on the dusty streets of Cuzco.

His features are classically Andean: oval face with high check bones and almond eyes, but his hawklike nose denotes royalty. His demeanor in Cuzco is that of a humble mountain Indian, but his bearing is proud. In his own land, among his people, he is a prince, treating everyone with respect as he is respected in return. Over the years that we have worked together, we have faced numerous physical challenges, but I have never seen him angry or display negative emotions, nor has he ever complained, even under the most difficult of conditions.

I say these things, not to paint an idealistic picture of a modern-day "noble savage," but to tell the truth. He is by far a better man than almost anyone I've ever known.

True, I've met others like him among the Eskimo in the Bering Sea, Athabascan Indians along the Yukon River, the Zapotec in Oaxaca, and the Shipibo in the Amazon. Perhaps genuine nobility is not found in kings and queens or modern politicians, but far from civilization and among people who practice a way of life and Earth-based traditions tens of thousands of years old. If the planet is to be saved from exploitation and ecological ruin, I don't think it will be by scientists or environmental activists, but by pure-hearted people like the Q'ero, much like the simple Hobbits saved the world in *The Lord of the Rings*.

I also work with Sebastian's younger brother, Jorge Palqar Flores. The two often perform ceremonies together, but work separately as well because they live in different villages, a distance of one day's walk between them. Jorge's character is less assuming than his brother's, but he is a formidable *paqo* and emanates a sensitive, generous spirit that I feel very close to. As the godfather of his daughter, Gloria, I am ceremonially bonded to his family.

Their father, Juan Palqar, was a highly respected *paqo* and one of the last great Andean shamans. Such men rarely come down from the mountains. Don Juan, however, was an exception to the typical reluctant Q'ero. He freely shared his knowledge and was beloved by many in Cuzco for his humor, generosity, warmth, and wisdom. Don Juan died in the mid-1990s. He taught the way of Q'ero shamans to his sons; now, Sebastian heads the family and carries on the tradition.

At the café, they sit silently while I review the menu, which includes trout dishes, chicken with Peruvian chilies called *aji*, and *loma saltado,* a stir-fry of beef, onions, and potatoes. I order soup with beef for them and *dieta de pollo,* a hearty chicken soup, for myself.

While we wait for our food, we talk. Sebastian wants to know how I knew the Tibetan monks, where they came from, and what I was doing in Cuzco. I want to know how they knew where to find me this morning, curious to know if it was coincidence or if they intuitively knew I would be there.

"Were you waiting long?" I ask.

"Not very long. Only a half-hour," Sebastian replies.

I should have known better. It was neither coincidence nor intuition, but synchronicity. They arrived as I arrived. The difference between us is that they know why they are there and are comfortable with the process. On the other hand, I am the typical impatient Westerner: continuously questioning, searching for meaning, and uncomfortable with a process that operates intelligently but is always just beyond the realm of my intellectual understanding. I have still to learn that nature finds ways to maintain links between us and the underlying or separate reality of the universe hidden from our normal waking consciousness.

The concept of a separate reality, to which we awaken through shamanic training, was written about by Carlos Castaneda starting in the 1960s. It has been recognized by

shamans, however, since the dawn of time. Once one's awareness of a separate reality is unshakable, synchronistic happen-
ings occur regularly and purposefully. This was the case with my
contact with the Q'ero. In meeting me, they were following
their natural way; the rest took care of itself. I eventually
accepted that one is always where one is supposed to be at
exactly the right time.

When I begin working with the Q'ero, I don't understand
this principle. I feel the need to explain things and tell Sebastian
and Jorge that I didn't know the Tibetans before meeting them
at Machu Picchu. I came to Cuzco to learn from the *Apus,* as I
had been instructed to do after my ayahuasca visions. They
comprehend immediately and I realize further explanation is
unnecessary. I feel ridiculous and, in the future, will not over-
explain myself to them.

"I am a *paqo* and *curandero,*" Sebastian informs me over a
bowl of creole soup, made with meat, vegetables, and eggs.
"We'll perform a ceremony for you to help clear the way for
your journey. Now we must attend to some sick people. Let's
meet tomorrow."

When they finish eating, they rise from the table as one.
Taking my hand, they thank me formally and sling their bundles over their backs. As they leave, Jorge looks over his shoulder and smiles, then they step through the doorway and vanish.

I sit alone pondering where this meeting with the Q'ero will
take me. Afterward, I walk to the library on Calle Ruinas and
read about Incan healing.

During Incan times, there were three levels of traditional
Andean healers. The *watoq* diagnosed illness through divination
with coca leaves, entrails of guinea pigs, or through visions and
dreams. The *hanpiq* was an expert in medicinal plants called
hampi, and treated common ailments with herbal and mineral
preparations. The highest level of healer was the *paqo,* who
treated soul illness. By returning balance between the body and

spirit through complex rituals, plant and animal medicines, and healing stones, *paqos* treat the cause of illness rather than alleviating only its physical symptoms.

Incan priests were specialists in ceremony and astronomy and they were organized into different levels, the highest being the *Willaq Uma*, a sage who could predict the future and cure illness with only his energy.

Modern Andean shamans assume the role of all three levels of healers. They also perform some of the former priestly functions. Therefore, they are best called shaman-priests. In Quechua, they refer to themselves as *paqos* and are organized in two levels: *altomesayoqs* and *pampamesayoqs*. These linguistic hybrid terms include the Spanish word for table, *mesa*. This is how Peruvian shamans refer to the altar on which they place ceremonial objects. These include stones, crystals, images of saints, various medicinal plants, *wayruru* and other seeds, red and white carnations or other flowers, and feathers. *Alto* means "high" in Spanish. *Pampa* is the Quechua word for "ground" and signifies a lower level. The suffix *yoq* in Quechua is used to denote possession. Thus *altomesayoq* means "the one of the high table."

A *pampamesayoq* is "the one of the low table." They are like general medical practitioners treating all types of physical and mental ailments, performing cleansing rituals to eliminate bad spirits, divining with coca leaves, and conducting ceremonies to honor *Pachamama*, the *Awkikuna*, and *Apus*. To become a *pampamesayoq* requires years of apprenticeship under a master shaman. It also involves months spent alone in the high mountains among the *Apus*. Sebastian is a *pampamesayoq* and has undergone rigorous training under the guidance of his father, Don Juan, and other Q'ero shamans. When it is time, Sebastian may assume the responsibility of an *altomesayoq*.

One doesn't become an *altomesayoq;* one is chosen. When a *pampamesayoq* is ready, the *Apus* select him or her by summoning the thunder spirit, *qhaqya*, to send a lightning bolt. The highest level of *altomesayoq* is one who is struck by lightning *three* times. The first bolt knocks him to the ground unconscious; the second bolt stops his heart and kills him; the third resuscitates him. According to Sebastian, there is only one living *altomesayoq* in Q'ero and few or none survive in other traditional Andean communities.

Early the next morning, Sebastian and Jorge are waiting for me and we begin the routine that I will become used to over the next four years.

"*K'uchi?*" Sebastian says. "Ready?"

We head toward the central market along the back streets of Cuzco. Sebastian and Jorge are a foot shorter in height than I. They wear their knit caps (*ch'ullus*) and plain gray and tan alpaca ponchos. Over his *ch'ullu*, Jorge wears a suede hat typical to the central Andes with equal brims on all sides to protect face and neck from the intense sunlight and a high peak to shed water. We walk briskly through the crowds that congest the streets and sidewalks. I follow, hatless, wearing a plain jacket, and am breathless from the altitude.

Cuzco's elevation is 10,800 feet and because of the altitude, the purity of the air, and proximity to the equator, Andean light seems as if refracted by thousands of diamonds. Its brilliance heightens the intensity of colors in their handwoven garments so that reds and blues, and even the earthen tones of Indian women's skin, seem so saturated with color that they appear to be photographically enhanced.

The market spreads out in a labyrinth of ramshackle stalls covered in sky blue and bright orange plastic tarps. In alleys so narrow we have to walk sideways to pass, vendors hawk produce. Garlic, and red and yellow *ajis*, a *Capsicum* chili species native to Peru, fill the air with their pungent aroma. Stacks of raw meat, mountains of eggs, and pyramids of tangerines assault my senses. Potatoes are everywhere; native to Peru and the staple food in the Andes, they're displayed in all sizes, colors, and shapes. Multicolored corn called *choclos* and a dark purple variety used to make *chica morada,* a traditional Peruvian beverage, are heaped on plastic sheets spread on the ground. Dried beans in a multitude of types and colors, pre-Hispanic vegetables, fruits of all kinds, and coca—all are for sale.

Coca leaves come in compressed bundles about the size of a small papaya, tightly wrapped in muslin, or are sold loose by weight. We buy a large green plastic bag full of the olive-colored leaves. A pinch of limestone or a sticky black paste made from the ash of quinoa mixed with tree bark is often combined with the leaves for chewing to provide a chemical catalyst that makes the active alkaloids in the leaves available for absorption by the body.

Sebastian explains the combination to me: "*Mama Coca* is alive and powerful. It's the ideal offering for the *Apus.* The paste and leaves together are *yanantin,* a sacred pair. Coca speaks the truth to man, reveals the unknown, and gives strength and health."

I learn that the quality, not the quantity, of the offering is important. Leaves are carefully sorted to select the most perfectly shaped and the largest. Coca leaves are also used for divination and Sebastian is an expert in this.

Over the years we are together and as I gain his confidence, Sebastian shares the secrets of coca with me. I learn that each leaf represents a quality of life. Different shapes indicate health, money, love and relationship, the weather, good and bad fortune, animals, and natural events.

Coca, the divine plant of the Andes and the most important ceremonial plant of the Incas, was so highly valued by the ruling classes that its cultivation was regulated and its use by the common Indian was limited. When the Conquistadors arrived, they associated coca use with Incan religion and tried to eliminate it. It is so necessary for survival in the high Andes and so intimately linked to the culture, however, that the Spanish were unsuccessful in abolishing its use.

The botanical family to which coca belongs, Erythroxylaceae, contains 250 species. It is native to the eastern slopes of the Andes at elevations below 8,000 feet. Here the climate is humid and warm, and sufficient rainfall occurs to nourish the plants. Normally a midsized bush, if left on its own, the coca plant can grow into a tree. Typically, coca thrives in warm, moist, frost-free valleys between 1,500 and 6,000 feet above sea level. The plant grows up to eight feet. The leaves are rich in vitamins, protein, calcium, iron, and fiber. The cocaine content of the leaves ranges from 0.1 percent to 0.9 percent; like the user, it tends to get higher with altitude. Diurnal fluctuations of cocaine in the coca leaf occur during a 24-hour cycle. Chewing coca also counters the symptoms of "mountain sickness" and oxygen deprivation. The daily dose of the average *coquero,* Spanish for "coca chewer," is around 200 mg—several large handfuls chewed over the course of the day.

In leaf form, coca does not produce toxicity or dependence. Its effects are distinct from those of cocaine, which is but one of more than a dozen active compounds in the leaf. When the main active component, cocaine, is extracted, it becomes a powerful stimulant and addictive drug. Authentic shamans never use chemically altered or concentrated drugs derived from sacred plants.

Indispensable to life in the high Andes, coca leaves are sacred and essential. Coca sustains life at high altitude. It wards off hunger, enhances endurance, improves overall tolerance to the environment, defends against the cold, promotes a sense of well-being, heightens the senses, lifts the mood. It opens the respiratory passages and increases the oxygen content in the blood. It has a mild local anesthetic effect and is applied topically to treat arthritis and injuries. When used in a ritual context, it can expand the consciousness and mediate between humans and the gods.

The immediate effect of chewing coca leaves is an acrid, slightly bitter taste that burns the tongue and gums. There is some discomfort from the initial abrasion of hard dried leaves against sensitive tissues. Then your mouth becomes numb. Almost immediately, however, you feel a sense of lightness and clarity. What was once labored breathing and fatigue due to the altitude becomes effortless. In my case, with a history of asthma, especially with physical exertion, the improvement in respiration is almost miraculous. I can breathe deeply. There is also an effect on the mind. Vision becomes clearer and thinking easier. Like the difference between an inexpensive radio and a five-speaker system, nature becomes more beautiful and magically alive.

Further downhill, Sebastian leads me to a side street where the shops of *curanderos* and *brujos* are clustered. We enter one not much larger than the inside of a car. Dark gray condor feathers hang next to the bright blues, yellows, and reds of macaws—birds now endangered and illegal to possess. On the walls are ocelot and other animal skins. Dried iridescent blue hummingbirds used to cure *el susto,* or "soul loss," hang in bunches from the ceiling. Red and black-eyed *wayrurus* used to attract good luck and ward off the "evil eye," scented waters called *agua florida,* religious relics, magical stones, resins for incense, statues of saints and Andean deities—all these are packed onto the narrow shelves.

The Indian woman who runs the place looks at me as if I am a long-lost relative she can't place. Children play among the things and some sleep like puppies curled up on burlap sacks full of dried herbs.

Sebastian selects ingredients for a *despacho*. The Spanish word *despacho,* as used in the Andes, means a ceremony of reciprocity. It is a sharing with the *Awkikuna* and a symbolic giving back to *Pachamama* for her nourishment and protection. *Awkikuna* refers to nature spirits that serve as protectors of caves, springs, unusual rock formations, large trees, and lakes.

The *despacho* is central to Andean beliefs. The entire Incan cosmic vision is represented microcosmically in the way the *despacho* is prepared. Gradually, over the years I work with him, I learn the significance and order of each component.

Sebastian handpicks dried grains and seeds, colored threads, metallic foil, brightly colored candy and other sweets, powdered metal, confetti, and other things. Then he points to dried lizards. "We use these to cure broken bones," he says, thus beginning the first of many lessons for me in the articles of healing and the methods of ceremonial work.

He chooses what looks like a mummified bird without feathers. As the shopkeeper wraps it in newspaper, he says, "Llama fetus for *Pachamama.*"

Over the weeks, I learn that *Pachamama,* like coca and potatoes, is all-important to Andean life. *Pachamama* is the great Earth Mother who sustains life and supports the spirit world of the *Apus* and *Awkikuna.* Without a relationship based on mutual respect and reciprocity to *Pachamama,* life for the traditional Andean is impossible.

Pachamama is not only the all-encompassing sentient being, similar to the Gaia concept, through whom we live and whom we share with animals, plants, rivers and lakes, the sea, and the mountains. To the Incas, *Pachamama* is both place and time. These are inseparable and occur simultaneously. For them, the Spirit dimension and the material world are interlaced. There is no separation of body and mind, as in the modern world, nor is there the fragmentation of the intellect and emotions. Life and death are different aspects of one continuous interwoven experience. The mythical dimension touches physical reality much as a painter uses a brush on a canvas layering colors to create an image. Likewise, space and time coexist in a continuum and are not separate domains. In this sense, Incan cosmology is more like quantum physics than Newton's paradigm of a finite, static universe governed by fixed mathematical rules.

This characteristic of inseparability of place and time together with the generative and supportive abilities of the Earth is what makes *Pachamama* sacred to the Andean. To understand Q'ero thought and garner insight from their way of life, it becomes essential for me to think of *Pachamama* not as the nourishing Earth Mother only but as Earth-time.

To the Q'ero, time is not linear. One minute does not precede another. Time is a process that spreads in every direction. It is multidimensional, interpenetrating the three worlds: *ukhupacha, kaypacha, hananpacha*. The individual is not the center of the universe but moves upon the Earth in the matrix of time.

Over the years I am with him, I learn from Sebastian that Andean mystical teachings are more than ethical and philosophical concepts. They derive from the living landscape. I come to know that when we listen, nature speaks. *Pachamama* communicates in an intuitive language that predates human speech but is nevertheless understandable to the shaman. Quechua, or *runasimi*, the language of the Incas, derives from the sounds of nature. Water running over stones, wind through the grass, birds warbling to each other. Nature's language is all around us. We have but to listen.

On a personal level, when *Pachamama* is approached in a respectful manner, routine consciousness becomes mystical. True, the thin air at high altitudes and ritual chewing of coca leaves facilitate this sense of otherworldliness, but fundamentally it is this ability to see the world differently, to acknowledge that a separate reality coexists, that distinguishes the Andean worldview from the Western.

The shaman uses his ability to alter states of consciousness to slip between "cracks" in Earth-time to enter this separate reality where the *Apus, Awkikuna,* and spiritual masters dwell. The highest initiations of the Andean sacred path involve transforming the initiate's consciousness through light. Being struck by lightning is but the beginning of the Andean shaman's journey, the path of light. The highest initiations involve transforming the initiate's material body into the light body. Eventually, after years of arduous training, the master shaman is capable of leaving the limitations of Earth-time and traveling beyond the speed of light. At the point of death, the Andean shaman's journey doesn't end. His luminous essence merges with the pure spiritual energy of the *Apus*.

How this is accomplished is a mystery. I have interviewed people in Peru who have witnessed shamans disappear and reappear in other locations, bring messages from relatives at great distances, retrieve lost objects, transport objects from one location to another, and have their physical body in more than one place at a time. The Incas called such a one *Intikana*, a being of light, limitless and at one with *Inti*.

As if reading my thoughts, Jorge says: "The Earth is our mother and the Sun our father. We are *Intiq churikuna*, Children of the Sun."

The lesson is over. Sebastian completes his transactions and we make our way back through the maze of vendors and crowded streets to the Plaza de Armas. We agree to meet later in the afternoon before the sun sets. To pass the time, I familiarize myself with Cuzco.

They say that if you understand Cuzco, you understand the Incan empire. A combination of the present and the past, Cuzco is tangible and elusive at the same time. It is buried in historical layers, embroiled in cultural and economic conflict, and populated by some of the most endearing people one would ever wish to meet. Paradox abounds here. Nothing is as it seems.

Creation myths reveal much about a culture and its origins. Incan myths of origin begin at Lake Titicaca in Bolivia but move on to Cuzco where the Incan civilization was founded.

In the beginning of Earth-time, *Wiraqocha*, the world-teacher who created all things, traveled from the sea and appeared over Lake Titicaca, the largest freshwater lake in the world, at an altitude of 12,500 feet on the border of current-day Peru and Bolivia. Walking north, he brought the world, still in darkness, to light. Once the universe and the planet Earth were ordered in Earth-time, *Wiraqocha,* the creator-god and androgynous tribal ancestor of all Andean people, appeared in human form and created the first Inca, Manqo Qhapaq. Entrusting Manqo Qhapaq with a staff of gold, *Wiraqocha* instructed him to found a city where the staff sunk into the ground.

Leaving Lake Titicaca, Manqo Qhapaq walked north until he came to the Sacred Valley of the Incas, a narrow stretch of fertile land between Pisac and Ollantaytambo. From there he discovered the high mountain valley where Cuzco would be established.

As the capital and center of the Incan empire *Tawantinsuyu* (the Four Corners of the World), Cuzco formed the axis of the Incan cosmological and geopolitical system. Each of four *suyus,* or regions, extended outward from Cuzco, which is spelled *Qosqo* in Quechua, meaning "the navel of the world." *Chinchaysuyu* composed the northern region and extended as far as Quito, the capital of Ecuador. *Qollasuyu* was the southern region including Bolivia and reaching into Chile and Argentina. *Kuntisuyu* composed the western part of the empire extending to the Pacific Ocean, and *Antisuyu* the eastern region that reached into the Amazon basin, into Brazil and the northeastern part of Peru.

Cuzco was divided into *hanan* (upper) and *urin* (lower) halves; these were further partitioned into various quarters. The two major halves established an east-west axis based on the observation of the rising equinox sun over Apu Pachatusan, one of the sacred mountains that surround Cuzco and referred to as "support-pillar of Earth-time from where the world spins." Other ritually important mountains include Apu Ausangate, a six-hour bus ride south of Cuzco, and Apu Salkantay to the north.

The epicenter of Cuzco was *the Qorikancha,* the Temple of

the Sun. It formed the center point from which radiated an elaborate system of lines called *seq'es* in Quechua. The spiritual landscape of the Incas, with Cuzco as its center, was composed of numerous *seq'es* with corresponding shrines called *wakas* that housed the *Awkikuna;* there are 41 *seq'es* and 323 *wakas* in the Cuzco area. The surrounding mountains and their *Apus* complete the sacred landscape of the Incas.

Wakas are naturally occurring but unusually shaped rock outcroppings, caves, and springs that serve as portals through which the spirit world influences the earthly. Incan stoneworkers often enhanced caves and outcroppings by carving seats and designs into the rocks. Some *wakas* were used as astronomical sighting points to mark important celestial events on the Incan ritual calendar. Many served as burial sites housing mummies. The Incas practiced ancestor worship and developed the skill of embalming to a high art. Mummies of the Incas were revered and housed in special *wakas* until the Spaniards destroyed them as part of their systematic elimination of all things indigenous.

Shaman-priests interact with the spirits at *wakas*. Through them the sacred connection that shapes the lives and destinies of the inhabitants of the local region surrounding a *waka* is maintained. In Incan times, specialists in shrines and sacred objects are called *wakamayoqs,* and *willkamayoqs* were employed to coordinate ceremonial worship. These often elaborate ceremonies included the ritual sacrifice of llamas. Routine duties like ensuring that appropriate offerings were made to each different resident spirit, however, were supervised by *wakamayoqs.* In modern times, honoring *Pachamama* and making offerings to the *Awkikuna* is carried out by *pampamesayoqs* like Sebastian.

I set out to meet Sebastian and Jorge around four in the afternoon. As I make my way through the narrow stone streets, I find them waiting for me a few blocks from the Plaza de Armas.

"This is a good place to start," Sebastian says.

We begin our walk out of Cuzco at the first *waka, Guaracince,* now a park and small museum. During Incan times, it was located in *Chuquipampa* or "plain of gold," next to what the Spanish called the Temple of the Sun. The *Qorikancha,* the Incan high temple to the sun and the most sacred spot in the Incan universe, is situated on a rise of land high enough to be visible from a distance and near the juncture of two streams that once flowed through the city, but are now covered over with buildings. Within it were housed the finest gold and silver objects kept in numerous shrines dedicated to the sun, moon, stars, thunder, rainbow, and *Wiraqocha.* The fabled giant golden disc was also housed here. The stonework is so precise it looks as if cut by a laser.

From here, we make our way through the narrow cobblestone streets to the Plaza de Armas. *Aucaypata,* as it was called in Incan times, is a place so saturated by history that the staccato beat of Spanish horse hooves can still be heard on moonless nights. The last Inca, Tupaq Amaru, was executed by Pizarro in the center of the plaza while the city wept. Later, four churches were built on two sides of the plaza. To the northeast is the main cathedral built in 1556 on the site of the palace of Inca Wiraqocha. Adjoining it are two churches: Jesus Maria built in 1733 and El Trunfo built in 1536, the oldest church in Cuzco. On the south side of the plaza is La Compañita, a church built by the Jesuits in 1668 on the site of Inca Wayna Qhapaq's palace and *Amaru kancha,* the temple of the serpents.

From the Plaza de Armas, we walk uphill through a residential area of colonial houses, many built upon Incan stone foundations and some with the original archways. Sebastian points to one that escaped the Spanish obsession with destroying anything with the image of snakes thinking them representations of the devil. Facing each other over a green door are two snakes carved in *bas relief* from stone. Could this be *Amaru marka wasi,* the seventh *waka* of the first *seq'e* of *Antisuyu* and former residence of Amaru Tupaq Inka?

As we stop at a vantage point above the city, Sebastian describes how Cuzco is shaped. Pachakuteq, the ninth Inca, designed Cuzco to look like a puma with its head touching Sacsayhuaman, an impressive archeological site made of gigantic stones, and its tail arching down Avenida El Sol toward the south. In doing so, he transformed it from a simple town into a sacred city. During the golden period of Incan history, it was known as the "City of the Solar Puma."

Large cats such as the jaguar and puma feature frequently as totem animals in New World indigenous lore. They are shy but fearless, fleet and fast, secretive, and as animals of the night, hard to see. According to Andean belief, a shaman has similar characteristics. The puma is significant because it is the largest cat in the Andes and most ferocious of predatory animals. Its power and fearlessness signify the type of energy needed for the Incas to expand and maintain their empire. Other important totem animals of the Andes are the condor, the eagle, the hummingbird, and the serpent.

Awakening the Puma, a ceremony that occurs on the winter solstice, is conducted by *pumarunas* (puma men), shamans dedicated to ceremonies associated with the puma. At this time, the beginning of the solar year, which occurs on June 21 in the Southern Hemisphere, the Inca gathered the court, priests, astronomers, warriors, and the people of Cuzco in the great central square at the site of the current Plaza de Armas to begin the celebration of *Inti Raymi*.

In the cold and darkness of the Andean early morning, thousands of people waited in silence for the sun to rise. Then, as the first rays appeared, a priest blew a conch shell signaling that the sun had touched the puma's head.

The appearance of the sun above Apu Pikol, a mountain to the east of Cuzco, signified the beginning of the creative cycle of spring. As sunlight fell progressively upon sacred sites, *wakas*, within the city, each was awakened in turn. Traditionally, it was believed that when it reached the puma's tail, the energy of the city and the empire was enlivened. At the moment of full sunrise over the city, the walls of the *Qorikancha* were bathed in sunlight and, within, the golden disc of the sun dazzled. This awakening of power occurred not only in Cuzco, but also to a lesser extent simultaneously all over the Andes as the rising sun illuminated *wakas* and temples.

The golden disc of the sun is central to Incan cosmology. It represents the sun's presence in Earth-time. So valued by the Incas, it was carried out of Cuzco to Vilcabamba, a mountainous jungle northeast of Machu Picchu, to protect it from the Spaniards. Legend has it that they never found it and that it remains hidden in the mythical or lost city of the Incas, Paititi.

Today, *Inti Raymi* takes place in Sacsayhuaman on June 24, the Catholic feast day of San Juan, Saint John the Baptist. Andean people still participate, and reenactments of former Incan ceremonies to the sun take place as a pageant, blending Incan traditions with Catholic. In the time of the Incas, Sacsayhuaman was an immense ceremonial complex and observatory. It lies less than two miles from the Plaza de Armas, which formed the ceremonial center of Cuzco, and is at an elevation of 11,800 feet. In the final days of the battle for Cuzco, Sacsayhuaman served as a fortification against the Spaniards. Its huge, precisely cut stones weigh as much as 350 tons each and stand as tall as 36 feet.

We climb farther to Sacsayhuaman, where we rest among the rocks. The late afternoon sun gives the otherwise gray stones a golden cast. Blue and yellow wildflowers bloom in profusion and butterflies and hummingbirds indulge in the last bits of nectar before sunset.

Sebastian points out where Incan stoneworkers carved seats in the rocks. Where we sit is a place for dreams and vision, he says. It contains seven windows that the Incan priest used for ceremonies to see the future. They are covered over with grass and shrubs, making it difficult to distinguish, but when I look carefully, I see that there are indeed seven stone shrines carved directly from solid rock or made from slabs evenly spaced around a circle. Though it has suffered the effects of erosion and neglect, the construction is arranged in a circle and set well below ground level. I will come back to this spot many times over the years for meditation and to contemplate the mysteries of the Andes.

Just as the sun touches the tips of the mountains, we proceed. Sebastian wants to take advantage of the remaining daylight and he leads us uphill to the southeast. This time I'm in the middle and Jorge walks behind. This pattern of walking will become our routine over the next several years until they allow me to walk in front. For now, I follow in the shaman's shadow as we make our way uphill past the stones of Sacsayhuaman and beyond to *Killarumiyoq*, the Temple of the Moon.

Qorikancha, the Incan high Temple of the Sun, was torn down by the Spanish and on its structure was built the Cathedral of Santo Domingo.

Example of precision Incan stonework in the *Qorikancha*

Incan stonework with two serpents carved in relief around the Spanish-made door in Cuzco

In the Cave of the Heart

Most Andean ceremonies are performed at noon when the sun, *Inti*, is at its zenith. However, those that honor the moon, *killa* in Quechua, occur at night and often during the full moon. In contrast to Incan sun temples, usually grand structures of huge precision-cut stone blocks, those to the moon are in natural stone formations or in caves. The Temple of the Moon, Killarumiyoq, above Cuzco is an immense rock outcropping set in the center of a large field as if it fell from the sky. It contains one main cave, and over the entrance is a fossilized boa at least 12 feet long and exposed in relief in the stone by eons of weathering.

Sebastian leads us through a fissure no wider than three feet. We carefully make our way along a narrow passage into the bones of the Earth. The stone walls are cold to the touch. At the end of the winding passageway, there is a circular stone altar about six feet in circumference and three feet above the ground. Centuries of ceremonial use have worn the surface glass smooth. Above it, a natural fissure allows sun or moonlight to illuminate the ceremonial section of the cave and causes the full moon to cast a single beam of light directly upon the altar.

Sebastian spreads his ceremonial cloths of deep red alpaca wool on the altar. He counts out sacred coca leaves, meticulously selecting the most evenly formed ones and those of the same size. Separating them into groups of three each, the grouping called a *k'intu,* he arranges these along the border of the wine-colored cloth. Then he takes from his sacred bundle a carved rattle, stones, and other ceremonial objects and arranges them to form a simple *mesa.* This is the personal altar from which a shaman worships *Pachamama,* honors the *Apus,* and assists in communicating with the *Awkikuna,* the nature spirits that populate the landscape and reside in *wakas.*

Q'ero *paqos* are very traditional, so their *mesas* are not as elaborate as those of Mestizo *curanderos.* Much like North American medicine men who carry the objects of their trade in a bundle that they keep by them at all times, Q'ero *paqos* carry objects they find in the mountains, that come to them directly from other dimensions, or that are given to them by another shaman. Years later, Sebastian gives me such objects for my own medicine bundle.

After sorting the coca leaves, he arranges the offerings we bought in the market on a sheet of white wrapping paper. He places gold and silver foil, the dried llama fetus, colored thread, confetti, candies, alpaca fat, garbanzo beans, corn, and other objects one by one in a pattern. He explains that by symbolic acts of reciprocity we honor *Pachamama* and show our gratitude and appreciation, or *agradecimiento* in Spanish, for life.

It is full moon and after the sun sets the cave is completely dark except for a funnel of moonlight coming through a fissure above the stone altar. As the moon rises in the night sky, the light in the cave becomes luminescent. When the moon is directly overhead, a single beam of silver light falls upon the altar at the exact spot where Sebastian has placed the offerings. This is what we have waited for.

The moon paints the walls of the cave opalescent. It is so beautiful and silent in the cave that I momentarily lose sense of where and who I am. Though the sense of timelessness is not limited to the Andes, it is very strong here.

With the concentration of an artist, Sebastian completes each detail of the *despacho*. When finished, he folds the white paper the objects are arranged on over the offerings and wraps the whole tightly in the ceremonial cloth. Grasping it in both hands, he holds it up to the beam of moonlight. Forcefully blowing into the bundle several times, he prays to the *Apus*, summoning the mountain spirits. I kneel on the stone altar. It is cold. He passes the bundle over my body, chanting in Quechua ancient words of protection and blessing.

Sebastian practices the art of his ancestors, a way that extends to a time before the Incas. The cave, within a giant, unusually shaped rock formation, symbolizes the womb of *Pachamama*. The round stone altar is a manifestation of the wholeness of creation and the roundness of the Earth and the moon. The darkness in the cave is the void. The spirit of the moon, *mamakilla,* is the grandmother of creation. The light of the full moon upon the altar awakens one's spiritual connection to *Pachamama*.

In the meantime, Jorge has collected firewood and starts a fire some distance away. After the moonlight ceremony, Sebastian and I emerge from the cave carrying the offerings still wrapped tightly in the paper and covered with the cloth. In the light cast by the full moon, we walk downhill into a valley to where Jorge has the fire going in a stone formation that looks like a chimney. After more prayers, Sebastian takes the paper bundle and throws it on the fire, the element of transformation. He explains that the offerings are burned in order to release their energy and, in this manner, the spirits are fed. The ceremony is complete and we make our way back to Cuzco in the waning moonlight.

In Incan times, this form of ritual worship of the *Apus* and *Pachamama* was elaborate. Such worship occurred on a prescribed basis according to the Incan solar calendar and to monthly lunar events such as the new and full moon. Participating in this ceremony, simple as it was, increased my bond with Sebastian and deepened my attunement to Andean ways. I felt he was preparing me for something else. By revealing his culture and Incan history, he helped me to begin to understand that the Q'ero place the Earth first.

The following morning, we meet again and walk to Q'enqo, another impressive rock outcropping situated between the Temple of the Moon and Sacsayhuaman. Though half the size of the Temple of the Moon, the energy it projects is impressive. Within Q'enqo's many passageways and chambers, one encounters what Andeans call the finiteness of individuality. Here, Incan priests invoked the dead and conducted ceremonies for mummification, a way of attempting to preserve individuality and defeat the permanence of death.

Before we enter, we rest on the grass. Sebastian selects a *k'intu* of coca leaves and, offering it to the *Apus*, prays for the spirits to help me understand the mysteries of this place. Then he shows me how to use coca properly.

"Choose three leaves without blemishes. The green side must face you," he says and arranges them in cloverleaf fashion. "Offer them to the *Apus* before putting them in your mouth."

He takes the cluster of three leaves, holds them tightly between his fingers, and blows lightly on them. *"Phuku,"* he pronounces, the Quechua word for the ritual blowing.

"We show respect in the same way before drinking water or *aqha,"* he says, pouring a small amount of the water I brought on the ground as a symbolic offering to *Pachamama*. I notice that he only touches the water bottle to his lips.

In this manner, he instructs me in Andean etiquette. In the years we are together, I will learn from his example that respect and reciprocity are the cornerstones of the Andean way. One offers food to others before eating. Before drinking any beverage, drops of it are sprinkled on the ground and before chewing coca leaves, one blows their essence to the world of spirits by performing the *phuku*. When done with respect and concentration, these acts align one's energy with *Pachamama* and the *Apus*. In this way, future problems are averted and obstacles avoided.

With the lesson complete, we lie side by side on the grass and look at the blue Andean sky. When rested, we enter the stone temple of Q'enco. Inside are passageways made luminous from light reflecting off the sand-colored walls. Incan masterwork is apparent in the meticulously carved altars and seats set high up along the wall of the cave. These subterranean passages are considered transitional spaces between the upper and lower worlds and have been used over the centuries for spiritual practices. Sebastian points to a carved niche high on one of the walls and indicates I should climb up there. I sit in meditation pose and concentrate to sense the energy of this place. He waits for me outside.

"In our land, the energy is even stronger," he says when I've finished.

After my meditation, I see Q'enco differently. I notice a number of stone steps that I hadn't seen at first. Each step is a series of three smaller ones.

"*Kaypacha, Ukhupacha, Hananpacha,*" Sebastian says, pointing to each step.

Each step represents one world in the three-world system of the Incan cosmic vision. The first step represents the world in which we live, *Kaypacha*. It also suggests the possibility of transcending the physical limitations of this world. The second step represents the interior world, *Ukhupacha*. Through dreams, death, and shamanic experiences, we find ways in which to enter the interior world. It is also the bridge between *Kaypacha* and *Hananpacha*, the higher world of spiritual beings and universal energy symbolized by the third step.

I didn't understand any of this on the night of my first *despacho* at the Temple of the Moon, or later at Q'enco. Gradually, over several years of working with Sebastian, I began to see patterns in his arrangements and in Incan stonework. As I let go of judgmental thinking and became more intuitive, I began to accept the possibilities inherent in Andean thought.

For example, in the symbolism of the steps, a common theme throughout the Andes, the three lines that form the horizontal edge of each step represent the Earth. The two vertical lines that form the outer edges indicate time. Together, with each step representing the three planes of existence, they symbolize the entirety of the Earth-time concept. The synergy between place and time is liberating rather than creating greater boundaries. Timelessness is the other side of Earth-time. Synchronicity takes place at the junction between Earth-time and timelessness.

We climb to the apex of the *waka* where Sebastian points out carved stones once used to record astronomical events such as the winter solstice. He shows me a zigzag, tadpole-shaped channel carved in the stone. At the time of the winter solstice, which occurs on June 21 in the Southern Hemisphere, the rising sun settles on the head, a round depression carved into the rock. Liquids, such as *chicha,* or the blood of sacrificed llamas, were once poured in the hollow forming the head and flowed down the channel making the body and away from the head. The pattern left by the liquid was read as an oracle to foretell the favorability of future events.

The sun is setting over the mountains. From the top of Q'enco, I look down on the red tile rooftops of Cuzco. The sky is clear and to the south the snowfields of Apu Ausungate turn golden and then a deep blue as the sun drops behind the mountains. Then we make our way downhill to Cuzco in the twilight. Sebastian is silent. I plod along behind him, lost in thought.

My experiences with Sebastian and the energies of the

Incan sacred sites form a new way of looking at the world. I am the same, but different. I cannot explain it. Years later, I would be able to put the pieces of each experience together like a puzzle. At the moment, the fact that the *despachos* and such places as these are of such importance to Sebastian convinces me that something good is occurring, something I should pay attention to and learn from. Slowly—it seems incrementally slow at times—I begin to understand the guiding principles of the Andes.

The next November, the end of the dry season in the Andes, I return. The seasons are in transition from winter to spring. Only the peaks of the mountains are covered in snow. Cuzco is colored sepia from dry grasses complementing the Earth tones of the adobe houses.

Sebastian meets me in the same inexplicable manner. I no longer have the need to rationalize how this happens and no longer feel that it is a mystery beyond my ability to comprehend. I accept that our separate lives in different parts of the world merge and, without planning, we synchronistically arrive at the same place at the same time. I begin to trust the process, and become more present in our work together.

This time, Sebastian is alone. We embrace. It feels good to be back. I invite him for breakfast at an inexpensive place near the market. He tells me about events in Q'ero.

"Jorge is working in the fields planting potatoes," he says. "The llamas are healthy and the children are full of energy."

We arrange to meet the following morning. I rise early and find him waiting for me. He tells me that we are going farther out of town this time and will need a car. Before hiring a taxi, we walk to the market to procure items for a *despacho,* including coca leaves. Sebastian wraps the items in his bundle. I hire a taxi and we drive about ten miles away from Cuzco and into the hills down a series of dirt roads that never receive repair, and finally stop at the edge of a rocky meadow. The high mountains that form the upper end of the Sacred Valley are visible in the distance. The day, typical for spring in the Andes, is warm, with thin white clouds scattered across a brilliant blue sky. The wind blows steadily out of the northwest. Occasionally, unexpected gusts whip up and are forceful enough to form little whirlwinds.

Sebastian leads the way across the meadow until we come to a stream. Typical of the kind that you find in the Andes, it is crystal clear, narrow but with deep pools, and bitterly cold. The air is cool, but the sun is hot and, after having walked for some time, I find the stream inviting. I express a desire to take a plunge, but Sebastian advises against it. The ice cold water, he informs me, will chill my body.

When in the Andes, it is not advisable to lower your body temperature, as the weather can suddenly and without warning turn icy. If one is unprepared for such drastic changes, hypothermia can occur. I heed his advice and only dip my hands in the water and rinse my face. Sebastian watches over me and makes sure that I don't drink any of the cold water, which he says can also chill the body. The Q'ero prefer to hydrate their bodies by drinking warm fluids such as teas and soups.

Once over the stream, we walk uphill across open rugged terrain until we stand above a shallow valley. Below us, and scattered along the valley, are large rock outcroppings, boulders, and clusters of gray stones carved long ago by Incan stoneworkers into seats and low tables but now overgrown with wildflowers. The valley lies along a *seq'e* and still holds a large number of *wakas*. In the distance, remnants of a few eucalyptus trees dot the lower end of the valley. Other than that, the landscape is covered in grass.

Sebastian points to one of the larger rock formations partway down the valley. "That's our destination. It's a beautiful place, very good energy, completely natural. You'll see."

Proceeding downhill, we move quickly over the uneven ground. Just above the rock, Sebastian slows and carefully descends along a narrow path that curves in a semicircle to the right and ends at the mouth of a cave. About 15 feet high and 12 feet across, the opening faces east. Pink and lavender wildflowers and small bushes grow around the entrance. Several large rocks with carved seats used centuries ago to watch ceremonies performed here and sculpted niches for ritual offerings are to the left of the cave.

We stand silent for a few moments. The magic of the place is tangible. Three white butterflies appear, first in bouncing flight, then in an orderly flight pattern. They circle my legs, fly upward to my chest, over my head, and then to the top of the rock formation. Flying in opposing circles, they spiral there for several moments and then do the same in the mouth of the cave before flying away up the valley.

Sebastian looks at me and says in his mixture of Spanish and Quechua, "It's a good sign. The energy is good. The *Awki* knows that you're here. It's a good day. It is beautiful."

As we become friends and he trusts that I am receptive, attentive, and respectful of his advice, I find that he often qualifies such moments with observations on how energy interacts between people and the environment. For him, out of the ordinary natural occurrences have significance. This day, in his opinion, is a good day for ceremonial work. The weather is cooperating, the wind calm, which is not always the case in the Andes, especially between seasons. As we arrive, the white butterflies appear. Such auspicious signs inform him that the *Awki* of that *waka* approves of our presence, and we can proceed with our work.

Drawn to where the butterflies had hovered at the pinnacle of the rock, I climb to the top. There is a flat spot large enough to stand on without losing my balance. I take out of my pack some Amazonian tobacco, *mapacho,* tightly rolled in a long cigarette. Lighting the *mapacho*, I offer thanks to the spirits of the valley and for the beauty of the day, and I blow smoke to the four directions. The smoke carries my prayers to the *Awkikuna* of the other shrines in the valley and the *Apus* of the surrounding mountains, and I ask their blessing on our ceremonial work. Gratitude fills my heart and I lift my arms to the sky and raise a voice to the Four Winds:

> *To the East, the place of insight and rebirth, I send a prayer.*
>
> *To the West, the place of death and wisdom, I send a voice.*
>
> *To the North, the place of clarity and cleansing, I offer respect.*
>
> *To the South, the place where Amaru, the serpent spirit, dwells and teaches healing and the spiritual powers of plants in the green place of reproduction and regeneration, I sing a song.*
>
> *To the Four Winds, I cast my spirit, open my heart, release my soul, and surrender to my destiny.*
>
> *Grant me the wisdom to understand the sacred in nature.*

After my prayers, I climb down and help prepare the fire. We had bought a bundle of firewood along the way, which I had carried, and now I prepare kindling and arrange the dry eucalyptus in a place of Sebastian's choosing just inside the cave.

He selects a place for the *despacho* on a grassy spot just above and to the right of the entrance to the cave. Here he spreads out his ceremonial cloth on the grass, prepares the ritual offerings, and pours out coca leaves. Andeans typically keep coca in a small woven bag that they sling over their shoulders. The strap is long enough that the bag hangs to one side within easy reach of their hands so they can take leaves out without effort. *Paqos* use a special fur bag made of alpaca fetus, called a *ch'uspa,* to carry ceremonial objects, and instead of slinging it over their shoulder they keep it wrapped in a carry cloth. Coca leaves are kept in the same bundle.

Sebastian selects the best leaves and puts the rest away. Then he arranges his objects and the coca leaves he has placed in several *k'intus* on a smaller cloth, forming his *mesa.* I offer him a *mapacho* cigarette, which he eagerly accepts. We smoke together in silence.

Though tobacco is native to the Amazon basin and widely used by shamans in the rain forest, as well as in North America, it is not commonly used nor is it a traditional part of Andean ceremonies. Still, in my experience, Andean shamans are knowledgeable about all plant medicines including tobacco and welcome "imports" from other Peruvian shamanic traditions when offered.

We smoke just enough to harmonize our spirits with the environment. After blowing smoke across the ceremonial space to cleanse it, we extinguish our smokes before we get drowsy. The beauty of the day and the sanctity of the moment still my restless heart. I sprinkle the remaining tobacco around the area as an offering for the nature spirits.

Sebastian carefully unwraps tiny packets of paper filled with sugary sweets, gold and silver foil, and other elements of the *despacho.* As he goes about his preparations, he comments on the "good energy" of the day and thanks me for the tobacco. While he completes his work, I finish stacking wood in preparation for the fire that closes the *despacho.*

When his arrangement is complete, he folds the paper over the offerings and wraps the packet in the small ceremonial cloths. While facing east, he blows three times on a *k'intu* invoking the *Apus.* Then taking his rattle and other sacred objects he prays to *Pachamama* and the *Apus.* He includes those in California, my home at the time. I stand and he passes the ceremonial bundle across my body, stroking down my arms and legs, then across my chest and back. He blows on the top of my head, into my cupped hands, and on other parts of my body to cleanse it of heavy negative energy and to impart the light, healing energy of the life-giving breath.

The cleansing part of the ceremony over, it is time to light the fire and burn the offering. This is done to release the energy within it for the spirits. It is the final act of the ceremony and signifies purification.

Sebastian straightens the wood to his liking, borrows my lighter, and lights the kindling. Flames immediately leap across the eucalyptus wood. When sure that the fire won't go out, he lovingly places the ceremonial bundle on top of the wood and we watch it burn. As a final touch, he pours the entire contents of a bottle of red wine on the ground around the fire as an offering to *Pachamama*. *Paqos* never drink liquor or wine but may drink, on rare occasions, warm beer or *aqha* if offered.

Sebastian comments again on how good the energy is today and points out to me how easily the fire caught onto the wood and how well it burned.

"The *despacho* was very good," he says enthusiastically. "The energy was well aligned today. Did you see how powerful the fire was, and how eagerly it consumed the offering? The *Awki* was very pleased. It's a good day."

I begin to understand his standards. Things and events have to line up. Weather, especially wind, rain, and hail, and all animals relay messages from the *Apus* and *Awkikuna*. Synchronistic events factor high for him. For me, it is like learning a new language.

I return to Cuzco in May (fall in the Andes) and, as usual, Sebastian is waiting for me. In the morning, he arrives at seven and we once again head into the hills above Sacsayhuaman. The pace is brisk and I have trouble breathing as I am not used to the altitude yet. I have to stop frequently and I fall behind. He waits for me at a stream with a narrow channel and deep bed covered with pebbles. Having learned my lesson the previous year, I don't even think about taking a swim and only splash my face. The icy cold water refreshes me. He watches, expressionless. Then we rest on a large stone at the bank of the stream.

"Today we enter the Earth," he says.

I take this metaphorically, but am wrong.

"It's time for you to visit *Pachamama* on another level. Soon we will arrive at a cave you haven't been to before and we will go inside."

We resume walking and shortly come upon one of many large rock outcroppings scattered over the area. I assess the rocks. At first glance, they are not particularly interesting, certainly less impressive than the others he has taken me to. Again, I am wrong. My lesson is significant and I am never again to take anything for granted in the Andes.

Leading me around a larger rock, he indicates that I am to go ahead. Pointing toward a narrow space between two boulders, he says, "Here's the cave."

I can't see an entrance. As I get closer, however, I see a narrow fissure in the gray stone. There is nothing remarkable about it and I am about to turn around when Sebastian motions me forward.

"It will be very dark in there. Be careful," he cautions. "We will be inside for some time until we reach the other side. I will be behind you."

I look inside, but can only see the first six feet before the passageway turns a corner. We go in. The walls are very narrow and my shoulders brush against the granite sides. Pieces of stone crumble and fall around my feet. My senses heighten and each piece of granite falling sounds like an explosion. From my experience, caves can start narrow at the entrance and then open into large chambers. I have been in several such caverns in Mexico and expect this to be similar. Wrong.

I inch forward into the cave. The darkness is complete, claustrophobic as a coffin. As the walls narrow even more and the ceiling lowers, my heart beats faster with each step. My small backpack wedges between the rock sides and I am unable to move forward or backward. Sebastian is so quiet that I have forgotten he is behind me. Anxiety takes over. Though I try to calm my racing heart by deep breathing, there is hardly any air and I feel I am suffocating. Sweat beads on my forehead. For a moment, panic charges through me like electricity. I am nauseous and dizzy, my mouth dry. I consider turning back, but the walls are too narrow to turn around and my jammed backpack prevents me from walking backward.

"Keep moving," Sebastian says from behind me.

Though he speaks quietly, his words sound like gun shots.

"I can't. My backpack is stuck."

I am wedged so tightly that I can't even move my arms to slip a strap off. I stop struggling and with extreme effort calm myself. I am unable to advance, but I can slide down. In a squatting position, I again struggle with the pack. Then, just when the situation seems hopeless, Sebastian lifts the pack up and slips one strap and then the other off my shoulders. He passes the pack between my legs for me to carry. I can turn to my side and continue sideways along the passageway.

There is no turning around now. The path descends and the farther we go, the darker it becomes and the staler the air is until it is nearly impossible to breathe. The darkness is absolute and I have no sense of direction. There is no up or down, only the void.

"We are deep inside the womb of *Pachamama*," Sebastian whispers. "Keep going."

I don't feel embraced. Rather, an overwhelming dread is taking me over.

His voice reassures me and I inch forward. My body makes scraping sounds against the rock walls. He moves in silence.

After what seems like hours, the walls widen and I can walk almost upright. Though still dark, fresh air comes at me from down the passageway and I gulp it as if it were a glass of cool water.

Before we come out the other end, Sebastian warns me that the light will be bright and that I should cover my eyes. I am so thankful to be out of the cave and eager to see the light, however, that I don't heed his instructions. When the sunlight hits my retina, it feels as if someone punched me in the head. I stagger backward and nearly fall over. Sebastian steadies me and we sit for a while on the rocks until my eyes adjust.

In situations such as I experienced in the cave, one is confronted with the darkest fears imaginable. If one survives, fear has less power, which doesn't mean one permanently conquers fear, as there are many aspects of fear and life is long. Afterward, if negotiated successfully, meaning can come in torrents. More often understanding comes slowly, the way twilight slips into night.

The next evening, the day before I have to return to California, we sit together in the living room of our mutual friend Jackeline. She is Sebastian's *comadre*, godmother, and I stay in her home when I am in Cuzco. He unrolls his ceremonial bundle and takes from among his sacred objects what at first appears to be a round stone.

"Keep this with you at all times in the Andes," he tells me seriously. "If lightning strikes you, it will protect you."

I turn it over in my hands. It is extremely heavy and not a piece of rock at all but a metallic object, which I take to be some kind of iron ore.

Then he hands me a large chunk of white quartz. "This is from my land, Q'ero. Keep this in your home and the energy of the *Apus* will be with you."

I return to Peru in March 2004. When I arrive in Cuzco,

Sebastian is waiting. We go to Jackeline's house and sit in the kitchen. The three of us discuss many things that evening, and many of the pieces of the Peruvian puzzle in my life begin to make sense.

The mysteries of the Andes have fascinated me since I was 15. I was enthralled by Leonard Clark's riveting account of his search for the Seven Cities of Cibola, rumored to hold a huge hoard of Incan gold. His book, *The Rivers Ran East*, was first published in 1953; out of print for many years, it was reprinted in 2001. In Peru, talk of Incan treasure inevitably brings up Paititi, the Quechua word for the lost city of the Incas.

"Do you remember when I took you to meet Jackeline for the first time?" Sebastian asks.

"*Hai!* I remember it as if it happened only yesterday," I answer.

Several years earlier Sebastian had taken me one morning to Jackeline's home in Wanchaq, a part of Cuzco, where she lives with her mother, her husband and two children, grandfather, and various extended family members. The home is colonial style and painted white with blue trim and doors. We arrived before the sun rose above the mountains surrounding the city. The streets were empty and people were only just getting up. Jackeline appeared on the balcony, and sleepy-eyed she stared at us with a puzzled, though attentive look. Sebastian introduced us and we embraced Peruvian style with a firm hug. She watched me the entire time I was there as if I were an alien.

The next time we met, she was cheerful in a relaxed manner that I was to learn was her usual personality. She immediately felt it necessary to explain her behavior of the previous visit. "I was still asleep when my *compadre* first brought you here. In the early morning, I had a dream. Sebastian's arrival woke me from my sleep. The dream was about you. When I saw you, exactly as in my dream, I was stunned."

I waited for details, but she didn't continue. Sebastian asked her to tell us more about the dream. We were sitting in the small kitchen around a wooden table painted light blue. She stopped putting dishes away and sat down with us.

"Sebastian and I, along with some other people, were on a mission to find Paititi in the deep jungle of the Vilcabamba. After what seemed like weeks of searching, we at last found the entrance. It was an unusually shaped portal. When we reached it, you were there already. We each asked you permission to enter. Sebastian went first. As we approached, you let each one pass until it was my turn. At the entrance, you and I stood and looked at each other. I looked at you for a long time, amazed that an Anglo was guardian of the entrance to the lost city of the Incas. I remembered your face in every detail. Then there was knocking at the door, and I woke up."

Sebastian nodded, acknowledging the importance of her dream.

"When the time is right, we must go together to Vilcabamba to search for Paititi in the jungle," I said.

"If you know of Paititi, you must have heard of the hidden monastery," she said.

Indeed, I knew of the legend. The monastery was rumored to be an Andean Shangri-La. I first heard of it in 1969 when I read *Secret of the Andes* by Brother Philip. Published in 1961, this book tells that the Lemurian masters took their teachings and a huge golden disc, the golden sun disc of Mu, to Lake Titicaca in Bolivia after the cataclysm that destroyed their continent in the Pacific. In a fabulous account of immortals, extraterrestrial masters, and a hierarchy of sages, Brother Philip claimed that remnants of these teachings are preserved in a monastery in the Peruvian Andes near the Bolivian border.

Greatly impressed by this account, I was compelled to search for the monastery and pursued this trail from 1969 to 1976, first in South America and then in Mount Shasta, California, when I met Sister Thedra.

In 1976, I traveled to Mount Shasta on the rumor that it was a spiritual power center. My intention was to spend time in meditation on the mountain; however, that never happened. Unexpected events detoured me.

I arrived late on a Sunday afternoon in the middle of July on the day of the full moon. Mount Shasta, a dormant volcano, was so spectacular in the sunset I decided to drive up the road that went to a ski area on the mountain to watch the moon rise. My old Chevrolet labored up the steep grade and, as I neared the top, the transmission blew. Without gears, I couldn't drive farther. Pulling to the side of the road and stepping out of the car, I watched the moon rise out of the eastern foothills. Then I pushed the car around and rode my brakes down the mountain into town and, miraculously, to the entrance of an auto repair shop. No one was working, so I left a note on the windshield saying that I would return in the morning and walked into town to find a motel. It took five days to order the car parts and install them.

While waiting, I frequented the bookstores and talked with local people interested in the esoteric. I was drawn to visit a well-known psychic whose card I found in one of the bookstores and, as soon as my car was drivable, I called for an appointment.

Immediately upon my arrival, she informed me that I was in Mount Shasta to meet Sister Thedra, a person I had never heard of. The psychic told me that Sister Thedra was in isolation, and no one, including the psychic herself, knew where she lived. At the time, since I did not even know who Sister Thedra was, I had no idea she had been to Peru. I slowly rose from the antique chair in the psychic's interview room, scanning her face for clues to help me, doubtful that I would find her on my own.

"I honestly cannot help you," she said empathetically but kindly, reading my facial expression accurately. "The only thing I know is that she is elderly and has chosen a cloistered life away from the public. If she wants to be found, you will find her."

Turning to leave, I politely thanked the psychic. I walked to my Chevy in her driveway and drove away with no predetermined destination in mind. I've always had a good sense of direction and a finely tuned internal compass, and as was my tendency in similar situations, I drove in whatever direction my intuition took me. This lasted an hour. Going down this street, turning here and there without any sense of what part of town I was in, I finally turned down a dusty unpaved lane on the outskirts of the town.

It was a hot mid-July day, and the dust from the street rose in clouds and hung in the air. The discomfort of the day, the inconvenience and expense of repairing my car, and the anticipated disappointment became unbearable.

Exasperated after driving aimlessly, I stopped the car, but kept the motor running. Overwhelmed with the hopelessness of my situation, I dropped my head on the steering wheel. An inexplicable calm descended over me and, looking up, I turned my head to the left just enough to see a cream-colored mission-style adobe house. I saw a long adobe wall enclosing a compound with the house to the left. Only the roof was visible. A small wooden door marked the transition from the outer wall of the house to the wall surrounding the compound. The tops of several fruit trees were the only other thing visible above the wall. To the left of the door, a bell hung from an iron hook and above it was a small white sign with black letters that read: "Mt. Shasta Abbey."

Simultaneously disbelieving that I could have "accidentally" driven to Sister Thedra's place and excited that I may have "found" where she lived, I walked to the door and rang the bell. A handsome, meticulously dressed young man with close-cropped hair answered. When I told him I was looking for Sister Thedra, he stared at me for a few moments before speaking, as if not knowing how to answer my question, making me think that perhaps he didn't speak English.

"This is Mount Shasta Abbey, but Sister Thedra is in permanent retreat and does not receive any visitors," he said formally.

I explained the importance of my visit, but he insisted that she was unavailable under any circumstances. He then apologized and was about to close the door when an overwhelming urge to tell him my situation compelled me to ask him to wait and hear me out.

Obligingly, but obviously impatient, he listened, but I could see that he was thinking of other tactics to get rid of me should I turn out to be a nuisance.

"Wait here," he ordered when I finished, then closed the door and disappeared behind the adobe wall.

I waited at least ten minutes, maybe 20; perhaps it was less, but it seemed like a long time. Just as I was about to leave, the door opened again. This time, a man about 50 years old, dressed in a tailored gray suit with the shaved head of a monk, appeared in the doorway.

"Good afternoon, I am Brother Stephen," he said politely. "I'm sorry, but Sister Thedra is unavailable to the public. She does not receive visitors and we make no exceptions, I'm sure you understand. She—"

He was interrupted mid-sentence by a woman's voice from behind the wall. Immediately excusing himself, he asked me to wait again and went back inside. From behind the wall, I could hear voices but could not make out what was being said.

Within minutes, Brother Stephen opened the door and, with a look of embarrassment, apologized in almost a whisper: "I'm very sorry, why didn't you tell me you had an appointment. Sister Thedra said you are late and that she's been expecting you. Please come in."

As surprised as he was, I tried not to show it and stepped behind him through the doorway into a manicured garden of roses and apple trees. Brother Stephen led me through the house to a large room with a long dining room table set with crystal glasses and white linen napkins. Pictures of spiritual masters hung on the walls, and the long half-drawn curtains that partially covered a large window at the far end of the room created an otherworldly atmosphere.

"Please wait here. Sister Thedra will be with you in a moment," he said and then left as quietly as he had first appeared.

Moments passed, then minutes. When more than 20 minutes had elapsed, I grew restless and got up to look at the various paintings. One attracted me more than the others and I immediately gravitated toward it.

At the far end of the room in an alcove illuminated only by the half-light was a black-and-white portrait of Christ. Once, years before in Seattle, I had seen a similar picture. Drawn in pencil by an artist in the Philippines, the complete gospel according to Matthew from the New Testament was written in such a way that it formed the image, much like the technique in Pointillism of using tiny colored dots. What made that drawing so miraculous was that the individual words were undecipherable unless you looked at it from a distance of an inch or two. The one on Sister Thedra's wall gave me the same feeling, and, at first, I thought it might be a print of the Philippine drawing.

Irresistibly drawn to the image, I edged closer until my face was within inches of it. But there were no words on it, and it appeared to be a photograph. At that moment, Sister Thedra entered.

"I was wondering if you'd find the picture. You took enough time."

"And if I hadn't found it?" I asked, turning away from the picture and walking to greet her.

"Then we wouldn't have had anything to talk about, and you would have had to leave," she informed me in a friendly but matter-of-fact manner as we shook hands.

We went to the picture and stood for some time about four feet in front of it, quietly admiring the delicate, wise, loving expression of the image. "It is beautiful, isn't it?" she said, more a statement than a question, breaking the silence.

Sister Thedra appeared to be a woman in her seventies, but she may have been older. I was 26. Like many spiritually evolved people I've been privileged to meet, her presence was of someone much larger than her actual stature. A slight but not frail-looking woman who had the color of someone who rarely went outdoors, she appeared in good health and walked nimbly to the table.

"Come, please sit down; I have much to tell you," she said, motioning me to sit down.

The younger monk brought us water and tea, and then left quietly.

"You are here to learn about the monastery, but let me tell you right now that you are not yet ready to enter it. You have much to learn and experience before you are ready."

Astonished at her knowing the true reason for my visit, I listened as Sister Thedra told me the story of her illness and the miraculous healing that had brought her to the spiritual path; her early training as a Western mystic; her five-year odyssey to Peru and Bolivia in search of the hidden monastery; how the photograph of Christ—whom she called Sananda—came into her hands; and how she came to Mount Shasta.

"In the late 1950s, several of us were chosen to travel to Peru to find the Monastery of the Seven Rays near Lake Titicaca. Unfortunately, there was disagreement from the beginning, and one individual who hadn't even been invited, George Williamson, insisted on joining our group. At first we agreed to have him, but later we asked him not to come with us. You see, he was a controversial person and we were not willing to jeopardize the credibility of our expedition because of this man."

She continued, "In those days, travel to South America was

difficult. We made our way by plane and train from country to country: first through Mexico, then Central America, and finally to La Paz, Bolivia. But before we arrived in the Andes, we already had our first falling out. While in Mexico, several chose to return and the rest of us continued. One person died along the way. By the time we reached La Paz, only five of us remained from the original 12."

Sister Thedra paused, looked intensely into my eyes, smiled, and then began her saga again: "One morning I went shopping alone at the Indian market in La Paz and woke up in the hospital more than a week later. My angels were protecting me that day and the Indians saved me. You see, I passed out in the market and when the Indians weren't able to wake me, one had the good sense to go to the hospital and inform the doctor on duty that a foreign white woman had died on their vegetables. But I hadn't died.

"When I was conscious, the doctor told me I had been in a diabetic coma for ten days. I hadn't even known that I was diabetic. Thinking I would buy a few fruits for breakfast, I had left the hotel without my passport. Without identification and in a coma, the hospital was unable to notify my friends. Later, back in the States, my companions told me that they had looked everywhere for me and, when unable to find me, became scared and fled Bolivia. Returning to the United States, they reported that I was either lost or dead. After recovering, I too made my way back to the States.

"And the monastery," I asked, "were you ever there?"

"The monastery exists, but by the time we were there it had already transitioned to a nonphysical plane and exists now only in a more rarefied dimension. The world is rapidly becoming more material and less spiritual. No place is truly safe any longer, even the heights of the Andes."

After a moment's pause, she continued: "When my companions returned without me, the leaders of our metaphysical group asked for a complete recount of the expedition. Williamson, who called himself Brother Philip, was there and he later wrote the book *Secret of the Andes*, mainly from what he heard at this meeting. He himself was never in Peru."

When she mentioned the name of the book, things began to make sense. But how she knew that I was coming, why I went to see her, without having a specific reason, and how she knew about my interest in the book and the monastery remain a mystery.

She excused herself, saying that she was tired. She wished me well on my spiritual journey, we shook hands, and she turned and walked into the other room. Brother Stephen showed me out through the garden where he paused, looked at me, and said, "I can see you like plants. Sister Thedra loves roses."

And, with that, I stepped through the door and into the dusty lane—my head a swirl of unanswered questions and the course of my life altered forever.

As I sat in Jackeline's tiny kitchen with Sebastian, I recalled other events that led me further on the path of discovery in Peru.

A week after my trip to Peru in 1996, I met Antón Ponce de León Paiva in San Diego while he was on tour promoting his books and soliciting funding for his center, Samana Wasi, a spiritual retreat and home for abandoned children in Urubamba in the Sacred Valley of the Incas. Samana Wasi is a Quechua word meaning "house of rest." In September 2000, I met with Antón in Urubamba. My intention was to discuss our mutual connection to Sister Thedra and find out what he knew, if anything, about the ancient spiritual brotherhoods reported to exist in the Andes.

Antón had met Sister Thedra in Sedona, Arizona, many years after I had seen her in Mount Shasta and only weeks before she passed away. He filled me in on details of her life that

I hadn't known. Sister Thedra was healed of cancer by the one known as Jesus, whom she later referred to as Sananda. After her recovery, she made it her life's work to transcribe the channeled teachings of Sananda, which are presented in her collected writings. Part of these teachings discuss a hidden monastery in the Andes, which she and a small group of spiritual adventurers attempted to find. Upon her return from Peru and Bolivia, she was guided to establish a spiritual sanctuary in the town of Mount Shasta in Northern California. After living many years in Mount Shasta, she moved her organization to Sedona, where she died on June 13, 1992.

Before she died, she requested that upon her death the picture of Sananda be given to Antón along with some of her ashes. Antón took me to a small rock garden where he had buried some of her ashes; the rest, he said, were scattered over Lake Titicaca, according to her wishes. After meeting Sister Thedra, he had wanted to dedicate a small garden to her memory. Knowing that she loved roses, he bought several red rose bushes and planted them in the rock garden. But the roses would not grow and, despite the best efforts of his experienced gardener, they failed, withered, and were all but dead.

Then one day, one began to leaf and bud and on the sole living bush, a red rose bush, seven white roses mysteriously bloomed. Later, Antón discovered that they had bloomed on the day Sister Thedra died. The roses lasted for a month and then that bush too died. It was in this garden that Anton placed the ashes.

Anton told me that the present-day organization of the Solar Brotherhood, *Los Intic Churinkuna*, was founded on the principles of Quechua culture for the purpose of promoting the teachings of the brotherhood as taught to Anton through his Andean mentors, described in detail in his *In Search of the Wise One* and other books he wrote.

Jackeline's voice brought me out of my reverie: "My cousin

searched for the monastery two times. The first time was only for three weeks. The second time lasted five months. He disappeared into the mountains and we thought he was dead. When he returned, he was different. His faced glowed for weeks. He hardly spoke. Then he told us that he found the monastery, but could never talk about it. Afterward, he got a job at a university in Denmark. He's been gone for six years."

I thought of the many people who have tried to find Paititi and the monastery. Some never returned, like the brother of my friend from Lima. The family still grieves his loss. She is hopeful he may one day return. No one has yet found any conclusive evidence that either Paititi or the monastery exist or if they are the same place.

Most of the time, Jackeline and I talked while Sebastian sat silent, his face expressionless. His reluctance suggested to me that the Q'ero, rumored to have information about the location of these places, may know more than they are willing to talk about.

Sebastian wisely allows me my thoughts. I ponder the implications of our talk in the kitchen, Jackeline's dream, my previous experiences with Sister Thedra and Anton. Is there a hidden monastery in the Andes? Does Paititi exist? Why does this theme keep reappearing in my life?

"I cannot answer these questions for you," he says, as if reading my mind. "You must travel your own journey."

This, I know, is the manner of Indians. Each one must live his own life, in his own way, walking his path in his own time. For them, life is a mystery to be lived, not a problem to be solved.

The conversation drifts away from speculating about hidden cities in the Andes to personal experiences. Jackeline asks me to describe my ayahuasca session, even though I have done so many times before. Then we talk about my experience in the cave. Though shaken by the experience, I tell them that there is one more cave I have to visit, the Temple of the Moon on the far side of Wayna Picchu.

When I finish, Sebastian and I look deeply into each other's eyes and we both know without speaking that I have to go alone this time.

"When you return, I will be waiting," he tells me.

Two days later, I take the train to Aguas Calientes. I have been to Machu Picchu several times and climbed Wayna Picchu, its sister mountain, but I have never been to the Temple of the Moon. Situated on the north side of the mountain, it is accessible only by a trail that at times barely clings to vertical stone cliffs; the cave that forms the temple is reported to be a mysterious place with many secrets.

It is March and still the rainy season. At Machu Picchu, everything is wet from the continuous moisture. At the start of the Wayna Picchu trail, I pause in front of the sacred rock of Machu Picchu: a large stone slab that mirrors the surrounding mountains, considered among the most spiritual of sites in the sanctuary. I pray for my safety and that the spirits assist me in my search for understanding my own heart.

The trail is slippery but manageable, and I proceed confidently. A pleasant breeze blows across the mountain. The steep slopes don't support the dense tree growth typical of the Amazon where the canopy creates a greenhouse effect holding in heat and moisture. I breathe deeply and feel energized by the pure air.

Forty-five minutes along, the trail forks and I take the one to the left. The right fork goes up to the top of Wayna Picchu, which served as an observatory in Incan times. A large white wild pigeon flies over me. As far as I know, no birds among the many that populate the area are completely white. I take it as a sign of shamanic resonance. No doubt Sebastian would say it is a spirit bird from the Other World come to greet me.

After an hour of walking, the trail becomes progressively

narrower and steeper. I pass sleeping platforms that Incan stoneworkers carved into the rock cliff. Moisture oozes from the stones and water spills off the walls in rivulets. I drink from one and listen to the sounds of a thousand drops.

On the northwest side of the mountain, the trail descends steadily and I soon come to the cloud forest. Small blue flowers of the lily family carpet the forest floor. Orchids and bromeliads cling to every branch large enough to support them and completely cover any fallen tree. The largest, *azucena de monte,* is not in flower; numerous pink epidendrums are about me. A blue-banded toucan lands in a tree near me and watches while I attune to the stillness and beauty of this place.

The resonance of Earth and sky, the harmony of day and night, the surrounding wilderness nourish the soul. I am a witness to God's creation. There are moments when everything and every aspect of my life come together and I sense a seamless order in all things. Today, this attunement lasts for more than an hour.

After so many years of walking in the Andes, I feel in my heart as if I am finally coming to rest. Clearing the heart, I realize, is the beginning of the shamanic path, the next step after being able to hear the magical language of nature and attune to synchronistic events. Though important, these three steps are only the beginning of the journey, not the end. But clearing the heart of the emotional debris of a lifetime is difficult. It requires visiting the darkest recesses of the psyche, as when I was in the cave the previous year. Fears abound in these places and must be removed one by one.

It starts to rain lightly. I drape a poncho over me and continue down the trail until I come to the Temple of the Moon, consisting of a natural cave on the lower side of the mountain. The Urubamba River is visible several thousand feet below as it snakes around the base of the mountains. Steep hills rise up on the opposite bank and many of them have cataracts spilling hundreds of feet in the air before falling into the river.

Inside the cave are five large and three small stone niches carved into the walls. Outside are sleeping quarters to the left of the cave and, in front of the entrance, terraced green areas where rituals were once performed. Inside is a basin for water shaped from stone and filled from the runoff above the cave. I look into it; it acts like a mirror. My soul is visible. My heart opens and tears drop from my eyes and mix with the water.

It's beautiful and quiet here, but I also sense power. As I move toward the back of the cave, my skin crawls and my breath quickens. Fearful, I back away. When I do, my respiration returns to normal. I think my reaction is only somatic memory from my earlier experience, so not wanting fear to control me, I try again. I experience the same reaction, so wait until after I perform a purification ritual before another attempt.

Returning to the mouth of the cave, I take from my backpack a Q'ero ceremonial cloth Sebastian gave me. I put tobacco on it, along with the stone from the Andes, flowers I gathered in the forest, and other ritual objects to form a simple *mesa*. I choose three perfect coca leaves (as Sebastian has taught me) to form a *k'intu;* standing, I do the ritual blowing and praying to the *Apus, Pachamama,* and the *Awkikuna* of this place. I light a *mapacho* cigarette and blow smoke over my *mesa* and to the Four Winds.

I sense that the spirits of the place are protective and might cause one harm if not approached respectfully. Taking coca leaves and tobacco, I walk again toward the back of the cave. I make offerings at each of the eight shrines and see that others before me have done the same, as remains of coca leaves are present in most of them. This time, I don't feel the unnerving sensations.

The back is a shallow cave and, though dim, some light still reaches it. There is a small shrine of stone. Ritual objects and coca leaves have been left on it by *paqos*. I offer my prayers, tobacco, and coca. There is no reason for me to linger, so I return to the front of the cave and sit in contemplation.

The previous four years of work and study in the Andes pass before me like time-lapse photography. I see the petals of my efforts opening one by one. Images of the Amazonian shamans flash before me, and I thank them, as if they were there in person, for all they have given me. I do not know when I will return to the Amazon and experience ayahuasca again, but I feel more prepared now. Lighter. No longer afraid.

I realize that the process of cleansing my heart has taken place effortlessly on its own while I went through the many different experiences with Sebastian and other Peruvian shamans. Now it is time for me to become more active, not a passive participant. At the entrance to the Temple of the Moon on Wayna Picchu, I make decisions that will affect my next decade. I will return to the Amazon later that year.

I struggle back in a heavy rain. The trail is slippery and dangerous, but I navigate it well enough and, once at Machu Picchu, catch the last bus of the day and ride down the mountain to Aguas Calientes.

The night is long but not uncomfortable and I sleep soundly in a small hotel. I dream that two small boas come out of the forest. One is green, the other blue. The blue one enters my mouth, slithers down my throat, and coils in my stomach. The green one enters the back of my skull at the top of the spine. It performs a type of cleansing of my brain that seems to take hours. When finished, it leaves through my mouth and returns to the forest. The blue one remains inside my belly.

True to his word, when I return from Machu Picchu, Sebastian is waiting for me in Cuzco. I feel different and sense that he knows this. I tell him only the highlights of my trip and we talk of my dream.

He listens but doesn't comment. Instead, he tells me about the high mountains of his homeland. Despite the harsh conditions, Sebastian speaks of Q'ero with pride and nostalgia. "There are streams of clear water everywhere. It tastes good and nothing is polluted with chemicals." His eyes, misting, drift over the landscape of memory and I can only imagine what he feels.

"What do you eat?" I ask.

"We grow potatoes without pesticides or commercial fertilizers. The ones in Cuzco don't taste good. Ours are natural and full of energy. My people have no cancer, allergies, diabetes, or heart problems. Everything is natural. There are no chemicals."

As he talks about Q'ero, I remember the many times he's invited me to visit his land. I always had an excuse not to go. I didn't have enough time, I'd tell him. But that was not the truth. I was afraid of what I might encounter there. But after my experience at the Temple of the Moon, I knew I could put it off no longer. My heart was guiding me and I had to go to Q'ero.

"Santiago, to learn more you must come to my land," Sebastian tells me. "In Q'ero you will understand what I have been trying to tell you all these years."

Temple of the Moon near Cuzco

Entrance to the cave inside the Temple of the Moon

Author and Sebastian in the cave inside the Temple of the Moon after the *despacho* on the full moon

Q'enco. The entrance to the inner passages are on the right.

Inside the inner passages of Q'enco

Valley above Cuzco situated along *seq'e* lines and containing numerous *wakas* like the high rock formation to the center right

Waka with cave where author and Sebastian performed numerous *despachos* for healing individual people and for the good of *Pachamama*

Temple of the Moon on the back side of Wayna Picchu

Sebastian prays as the sacred bundle burns to release its energy. This *despacho* is near Q'enco.

The Way of Love and Beauty

The first principle of the Andean way is called *munay* in Quechua. It means to love. I do not mean romantic love but a deep, abiding, impersonal love that comes naturally from the heart. This loving does not expect anything in return, but simply radiates emotional warmth and caring. It is a love of acceptance. When one loves in this manner, thoughtfulness and kindness follow as a rainbow follows rain. I think of it as lovingkindness.

Munay not only means a nourishing, all-encompassing love, but also signifies tranquility and beauty and suggests a pleasant experience characterized by harmony, symmetry, correctness, and tranquility, within and without. Beauty is the outer wrapping of *munay;* inside is kindness and love. To the Q'ero, beauty and love are inseparable. When you have these in your heart, you are peaceful.

Munay is inherent in nature. Not only does it manifest through nature as in a stunning sunset or a luscious fruit, it is also a quality within us. When both outer and inner worlds reflect love and beauty, one manifests benevolence in action and character.

In my experience, indigenous people like the Q'ero innately express this form of love. Perhaps this is because they are closer to the source of life. Other tribal groups in the Americas whose lifestyle remains much as it was a thousand years ago, such as the Yupik Eskimos, are much the same. It is not the same, however, for modern Westerners or for indigenous people who have had decades of contact with contemporary lifestyles.

To experience *munay*, we must cultivate it through conscious acts of kindness. Though one can work at clearing the heart, it is impossible to possess *munay*. When the time is right, *munay* manifests; like a hummingbird is attracted to blossoms, it comes when the field is fertile. It comes like grace. When *munay* becomes an integral part of one's character, it expresses itself spontaneously. For it to exist in this state, however, it is first necessary to clear the heart.

Over the years of working with Sebastian, I came to accept that deep, lasting change occurs in stages. In fact, it may take a lifetime to clear the heart. In essence, it is a return to a natural state of being. Then *munay* is present. In this way, I discovered that being patient with myself, but also honest, is itself a form of lovingkindness.

As my experiences in the Andes deepened, I was also learning, at times more painfully than others, that clearing my heart was not an easy task. The psychological burden of accumulated emotions and the memories attached to them can cause confused thinking and clouded judgment. It was necessary for me to feel emotionally free of my past, a prerequisite for *munay* to exist in me and be expressed in my actions. My experiences in the Andes helped shape me, and as a sculptor chisels a work from stone, the final form does not come easy. It will not be rushed.

Two months after my experience at the Temple of the Moon at Wayna Picchu, I am back in Peru. I know in my heart that I am ready to make the journey to Q'ero.

I left my world behind in stages. I flew from California to Lima, then from Lima to Cuzco, where Sebastian and Jorge are waiting. The next day, after more than four hours over a switchback dirt road on a rickety bus, we arrive at Paucartambo.

Along the way, the driver navigates the endless turns with precision, but still the edge of the bus is often inches from sheer drops of hundreds of feet. At other times, it rocks in and out of potholes deep enough to hide a pig and with such violence that passengers are thrown around inside. Miraculously, we arrive without a mishap, but none of the passengers sit in the seats they started out in.

Paucartambo is a small town of white colonial buildings that look like they haven't seen renovation since Spanish times. In the center of town is a square and to get there we cross an Incan bridge over the Mapacho River; the bridge is wide enough for a large truck to cross. In continuous use for at least five hundred years, the stones of the bridge seem to be fused into the riverbank.

We don't get to sleep until after ten and then awaken in the dark at four in the morning after a cold night sleeping in our clothes in a seedy *pensión*. We board an open truck packed with trade goods and Indians. It labors uphill for three hours on a trail so narrow vehicles can go up only once a week and have to return the next day. It is well below freezing and the wind adds a chill factor that claws its way through the panels on the truck and into my bones. The Indians bundle themselves in their ponchos and stoically endure the cold. The ride is extraordinarily uncomfortable. I'm stacked in the truck along with bundles and crates of supplies and it's impossible to adjust my position. Like the Indians, I hunker down to ride it out.

We reach a small village that serves as a market center for the area and a trail head for the Q'ero. Even though I am dressed in a down coat with the hood up and buttoned around my neck, have wool gloves on, and a wear a good pair of hiking boots with wool socks, I am very cold. The sun takes its time rising over the surrounding hills, but when it does, the air warms quickly.

By eight, the Q'ero pack four horses brought down from their village by Sebastian's youngest son, Rolando, who at 12 years old has already mastered many of the survival skills necessary for life above 14 thousand feet.

Under a cloudless sky, we leave the village behind and make our way along an Incan road through a valley of wildflowers. A clear stream runs through it on our left. Cream-colored llamas graze on the hills. Thankful to be out of the cold, I take off my down coat and gloves, regaling in the warmth of the morning sun. I walk leisurely along with the Q'ero, unaware that we are gradually moving uphill. As the elevation increases, so do my difficulties.

At first the walk is easy, but I find breathing difficult. By nine, my hands and feet swell. By ten, my head throbs unmercifully. I have underestimated the altitude and it is taking an early toil on my unaccustomed body. Even though I have considerable physical endurance and am in good health, I am concerned about the altitude. My swollen feet chafe against the sides of my boots and I have to stop by the stream to soak them in the icy water to slow the inflammation.

In sharp contrast to my physical discomfort, the morning proceeds as beautifully as it began. The horses behave. Everyone is in a good mood.

Along the way, Sebastian comments in Quechua, "*Munaycha.* It's so beautiful."

He is right: the sky, a cerulean blue, is nearly cloudless; the walls of the valley are covered with tall grass interspersed with countless wildflowers. The beauty eclipses my pain. My emotions soar even though my body aches. For a few hours, harmony reigns and everything is right with the world.

We continue along the Incan road until it separates into

three narrower trails. Taking the one to the left, we soon come to another Incan bridge. Serpent Bridge, *Chaka Amaru*, not much wider than a single person can pass comfortably, spans a deep ravine. Far below, a stream funnels along through the rock bed at an enormous speed.

On the other side of the bridge, the trail turns into a footpath and within a few miles disappears. This is the edge of Q'ero territory, a trackless place into which few outsiders have ever ventured.

Myths surround the Q'ero. Folk stories say that the people of Q'ero consider themselves ancestors of the Incas and took to the high mountains to escape repression and enslavement by the Spaniards and conversion by the Catholic Church. Perhaps, as some say, they are ancestors of Incan priests and royalty. Tales suggest their ancestral connection to Inkari, the legendary Inca who many believe will return one day to restore the Incan empire to its full splendor. The Q'ero moved enormous caches of gold and silver from Cuzco away from the Spanish to the Madre de Dios, a region of thick jungle believed to conceal Paititi, the lost city of the Incas—so the legends say.

To the Q'ero, the truth is simpler: This is their land, the place where they have always lived. They were here before the Incas. They endured the Spaniards, the cruel hacienda system, and the Peruvian government. When I've asked them how long they have lived here, they say that their people have lived there for "more than 1,000 years." This is their way of saying "forever."

In a group of eight agricultural and herding communities to the southeast of Cuzco, the Q'ero people weave, grow potatoes, and raise llamas, sheep, and alpacas at elevations of 14,000 feet and higher. The Q'ero say they have kept their independence from Spain and Peru and are an independent nation.

Throughout the Andes, the Q'ero are legendary. Considered to have maintained the purest form of the ancient way from before the Incas, they have the most adept *paqos*. The Q'ero embody the message of the Andes. These simple people, living in isolation for centuries and under the most primitive of conditions, may represent the last of what was noble in the Indians of all the Americas. To lose our sense of what is noble and good may be far worse than the extinction of a species of animal or plant. What is most human and good in people is *munay*.

Around noon, we stop on a grassy knoll to rest. In front of us, immense hills rise up directly in our path. Sebastian and his sons unpack the horses, who put their heads down and graze on the abundant grass.

Four hours into the journey and so far the Q'ero have not eaten or drunk anything other than hot soup in the early morning. Neither do they carry food or water. They spread their ponchos on the grass and lie down; later, we chew coca leaves.

"*Munaycha*," Sebastian says.

He smiles broadly and, in agreement, the others smile too, revealing perfectly white straight teeth.

I would have to be blind not to recognize what he means. Natural beauty surrounds us, wraps us in splendor, and draws us into its silence and peace. In that moment, I begin to understand that the shaman's path is not about the mind but the heart.

After about 30 minutes, the Q'ero repack the horses and we continue the journey. Along with us is Lorenzo, Sebastian's brother-in-law, and his two younger sons, Guillermo and the youngest, Rolando, who helps with the horses. Lorenzo, a sturdy man in his mid-thirties, wears tattered Western clothes but retains the colorful knitted cap, as if to let the outside world know that in his heart he remains Q'ero.

Though not traditionally a part of Andean culture, horses have been used since they were introduced by the Spanish at the time of the Conquest. The Q'ero still cling to a self-sufficient pastoral and agricultural existence and can survive without any outside support or supplies of any kind, yet since the mid-1990s some families have supplemented their diet of potatoes and alpaca meat with dried wheat noodles, cooking oil, salt and sugar, and, when they can, vegetables like carrots and onions. Horses or llamas are used to pack these supplies into the villages every few months. They are also used to carry firewood—there is none at the elevations at which the Q'ero live—and potatoes from the fields.

Lorenzo asks me if I want to ride, but I decline. I am determined to walk the entire distance with them. Within an hour, however, the going is difficult. As we gain altitude, my hands and feet swell more and, within a few hours, they are three times their normal size. My head throbs from cerebral edema and I am nauseous. I have been at altitudes up to 14,500 feet without symptoms of *soroche* (mountain sickness). But this is above 15,000 feet and we are to go to even higher elevations in the following days.

As a doctor, I know that my body is not adapting rapidly enough to the altitude. Acute symptoms of *soroche* can occur above 8,500 feet and include swelling of the brain, difficulty breathing, nausea and vomiting, insomnia and frequent wakening at night, heart palpitations, weird dreams, and lack of appetite. When severe, it can cause death from pulmonary edema, the collection of fluid in the lungs.

Despite the increasing altitude, the Q'ero maintain a steady pace and we cover a considerable distance over the next hour. The grade steepens to 45 degrees and the difficulty of the terrain for me increases by the minute. They continue without letting up until we reach a high knoll with a view of the terrain we had covered. The landscape has changed completely from rich agricultural terraces to wilderness. There are no trees or bushes and everything is uniformly colored a rich sepia due to the dry grass that covers the land. Unusually shaped boulders and giant rocks litter the landscape and remind me of my ayahuasca vision.

Far to our left, a river accompanies us. Blocking our path to the front, the knoll drops off into an immense ravine. Clouds and mist rise up from the deep valleys below. Drifting like curtains, when they part, they reveal high ragged mountains beyond. One in particular looms over the ravine like a giant sentinel. We have arrived at the entrance to the fabled land of Q'ero.

We stop here and rest again. Sebastian settles on his poncho, as do the others, and he spreads out coca on a cloth. Selecting three large evenly shaped leaves, he forms a *k'intu* and, standing, faces the mountain and prays. First, he performs the *phuku*, blowing the life force in his breath out to the *Apus*. Lorenzo does the same. The boys watch. I follow by making my own *k'intu*, then offer my prayers to the mountain spirits, thanking them for the opportunity to be with them and asking for guidance. Then we chew coca leaves.

This time my companions do not unpack the horses. We rest on our ponchos for about 20 minutes. More comfortable now as my symptoms have subsided, I watch the clouds and mist weave between the mountain peaks until we are ready to go on.

"*Munaycha*," Sebastian says again. Pointing to each mountain, hill, and stream, he gives their names in Quechua as if introducing his family.

Sebastian is undergoing a transformation. His face, radiant with love for this land, no longer has that submissive look he used in Cuzco: He looks now like a warrior. In Cuzco, he is a humble Indian who never speaks unless first spoken to, who keeps his head bowed. As we draw closer to Q'ero, he opens like a flower in the morning sun. By the time we reach his village, he will have become a prince among his people.

"*Munaycha* means *bonito*," he tells me. "Beauty."

Sebastian points to his chest. "When the heart is not tranquil, the mind becomes agitated. Clear your heart. Free your mind." He points to the surrounding mountains and looks off toward the northeast. "Soon we come to Q'ero."

I take him to mean that we are leaving civilization behind and to carry the emotional and mental baggage of modern living with me is not good. Later, I learn from him that the Q'ero believe symptoms of a restless mind include insomnia and, when severe, mental and emotional problems like forgetfulness. The Q'ero also consider most negative states of mind, such as greed or envy, moral concerns and emotional sickness, rather than psychological states or character traits. *Munay* is the natural human state of being. Deviations from mental and emotional harmony result in negative emotions which can cause disease.

What he says makes sense. I think about the struggle we Westerners go through in spiritual practice to arrive at this state. To elevate our consciousness and achieve peace, we undergo daily meditation, sitting for hours at the feet of a master, and read books on religion and psychology. Ironically, what Sebastian talks about may be the natural state of consciousness rather than a "higher" one. Perhaps we have been on the wrong road. Maybe to achieve enlightenment we need to let go of striving. It may be enough to clear our hearts and follow the example of nature by expressing beauty while manifesting strength and power within. No book can teach that.

Though few are born with an abundance of love and heart-centered awareness, it can be cultivated. Praying sincerely is one way to cultivate the energy of the heart. By doing this, we acknowledge a greater power than ourselves, one that is universal and all-loving. Being close to wild nature is another way. Learning to love ourselves more is yet another way to cultivate spiritual love. Most of us have gone through a time in our lives when our self-worth was low. Some experience this daily. When we do not love ourselves enough, we can become caught in self-destructive behavior or in relationships that are not supportive and loving. It is hard to love others if you don't love yourself. Caring for others or animals and plants is another way to cultivate *munay*. When love transcends personal fears and self-imposed limitations, it is liberating and is accompanied by joy.

In the years that I have known him, Sebastian has demonstrated lovingkindness and benevolence in all that I have seen him say and do. Expressing thanks for every moment and the gifts given, his affection is boundless. At times, he hugs and kisses me with such affection that it is almost embarrassing. Never taking advantage of his friends with whom he often stays on his infrequent trips to Cuzco, he inevitably waits for an invitation, even though he knows he is always welcome.

As he speaks, I experience peace. I sense the power of nature pulsating all around me. The landscape is alive.

I am awakened from my reverie when everyone gets up at the same time to ready the horses. The clouds have cleared enough to reveal an even higher mountain.

"There," Sebastian says, pointing to the peak. "We are going over that mountain."

In half an hour, we reach the base of the peak. The Q'ero encourage me to mount a horse. At first, I think we will circumnavigate the peak because it is so steep. They point out a barely visible trail, however, winding through a field of loose gray shale. Once I realize the way is up rather than around, I mount a dark brown horse and we begin the ascent.

The trail is so narrow the horses have to place one foot in front of the other. Andean horses, a type of Peruvian Paso horse descended from the Spanish horses of the Conquistadores and reported to have the smoothest gait of any breed, are bred for this type of high-altitude climb and narrow trails: They can walk on a line not much wider than their hooves.

The trail crosses the shale field and pieces slip under the horses' hooves. Slowly and carefully, they labor up the slope, near vertical in places, toward the summit. The air, thinning by the minute, makes it increasingly difficult to breathe and, for the first time on the trek, I am glad to have the assistance of the horses. The going is extremely difficult, however, and more than once a horse falters.

As we approach the summit, the trail is treacherous. I look over the edge to the base of the mountain thousands of feet below.

"If your horse falls, it will certainly be killed," Rolando says.

I get the point. If the horse falls with me on it, I will be killed as well. Later, at the bottom, to make his point, Rolando points out the jumbled bones of a horse that had fallen. The black mane and tail are still growing, it seems, out of the bleached bones.

At one point, the trail becomes so dangerous I dismount and go the rest of the way on foot. It is so steep in places that this is more like rock-climbing than hiking. We struggle upward. At the top, we pause, which I learn is their custom on such climbs. Below us is Q'ero, the land of mist and clouds. Large banks of fog move across the terrain like white dragons. Behind us is the sunny valley we just crossed. We begin the descent on foot.

The way down is as difficult as the ascent, but it's shorter. The horses have a more challenging time as they need to adjust their weight with each step to avoid falling. At the bottom, there is no trail, but the Q'ero move across the landscape like shadows.

We have not eaten and the two small bottles of water I brought with me are long gone. The Q'ero are impervious to the absence of food or liquids and continue on, even though we have three hours of hard walking to go. Their stamina is so great and their desire to get home before dark so strong that the closer we get to the village the more energy they seem to have.

We cross a rolling plateau cut with rivers and streams. As the sun sets behind the hills, we negotiate a rise in the land. A cluster of mountain peaks looms up behind the rise. The Q'ero quicken the pace to take advantage of the remaining light and we arrive at the base of another immense hill in the twilight.

Sebastian points upward, "My village is up there."

We labor on and, just as it is getting dark, arrive at a cluster of barely visible stone huts. Lorenzo unpacks the horses and lets them loose to graze. We enter a hut. Sebastian welcomes me to his community with a bowl of hot potato soup and a pile of boiled potatoes that are not much larger than my thumb.

"This is our home," he says, passing me another bowl of soup after I finish the first.

I am more exhausted than hungry and, noticing this, Lorenzo spreads clean dry grass on the dirt floor, covers it with a horse blanket, and invites me to lie down. He and his companions are ravenous and eat like they haven't seen food in weeks. They pass me more potatoes, and encourage me to eat.

"It's very cold here," Sebastian says. "The high altitude can reduce your stamina. If we don't eat potatoes, we can't walk far or work hard in the fields. Eat."

I look at my watch. The trip, if you could call it that, felt more like a forced march of guerrillas chased by government forces. It took ten hours. Later, Lorenzo, who works as a porter on the Inca Trail during the tourist season of July and August, tells me that the highest pass on the trail is at 13,800 feet. The one we crossed coming into Q'ero is close to 16,000 feet. Their village is at 14,000. A week later, we will cross passes higher than 18,500 feet.

As soon as everyone has eaten, alpaca skins are spread on the dirt floor and all lie down to sleep. The household consists of 12 people including adults and children. If they sleep pressed to one another, there is just enough floor space for each. During the night, none toss and turn, snore, or make the slightest sound. They sleep the restful, restorative sleep of infants.

Exhausted, I fall immediately asleep. But in the dead of

night, I awake to the sound of my heart beating. The darkness inside the hut is complete. No one stirs. There are no bird or insect sounds, and it is eerily silent. I am disoriented and, for a moment, panicky. I realize that it's the altitude making my heart labor. Breathing comes in gasps and I have to sit up. Then my respiration is easier and my heart rate normalizes. This is to become my sleeping pattern in Q'ero: two hours asleep, one hour sitting up, repeated through the night. I am envious of their ability to sleep deeply.

In the darkness, I feel as if I am in the womb of *Pachamama*. Brilliant streams of light flash around the hut. This lasts but a few seconds, but I feel I am witnessing the birth of the universe. Every night, all life is renewed like this and the world is born again in the day. With this, I fall back asleep.

Author and Q'ero Indians leave Paucartambo behind.

We dismount and proceed on foot to cross the main pass before arriving in Q'ero.

We enter Q'ero, the land of mist and clouds.

Esparilla, Sebastian's village

The Way of Knowledge

We awake in the cold. Despite the below freezing temperature, I am curious to see what the village looks like and, crawling through the tiny door of the stone hut, I go outside. In front of me spreads a white landscape. During the night, the mist settled and now covers the ground with a thick frost. The moon, nearly full, is setting over the hills. This first morning is unearthly: If not for the cold, which drives me back under the blankets and furs, I would sit outdoors for the sunrise.

The Q'ero are still under their furs and blankets. I burrow back into my sleeping bag to sleep. When I wake, I find that though the swelling of my hands and feet has normalized during the night, and my headache is gone, my enlarged feet had rubbed against my boots during the trek and pieces of skin all across my heels are gone, revealing raw flesh. My socks, stained with blood, are stuck to my heels. My feet throb and it is painful to move them. I will not walk for several days until they heal.

The intense cold keeps everyone under their covers, except the women who are tending the fire and boiling potatoes. Typically, they rise at four and begin a two-hour process that they repeat three times a day. It starts with making a fire. Then they cook large quantities of food in a few pots; it is labor intensive and time consuming. The fireplace is a stone and mud affair built on the ground. There is no chimney and the smoke from burning dried llama dung, the main source of fuel, is thick. It reluctantly vents through the grass roof but more seems to stay in the house than goes out. The smoke is so acrid that my eyes and the inside of my nose burn. The women seem accustomed to it and, oblivious to the smoke, they cook with a passion fueled by the need to feed a dozen hungry people.

From my sleeping mat, I observe that the living conditions are decidedly primitive but functional. In most ways, the lifestyle of the Q'ero has changed little since the Stone Age. The hut is a rectangle built of volleyball-size stones held in place by a mixture of mud and grass. The roof is a series of thin poles covered with grass. There are no windows and there is only one door of crude wooden slats hinged with alpaca hide strips; it is barely large enough for an adult to squeeze through. The dirt floor is hard-packed and dry, but uneven and slopes into the corner where I sleep; it is covered with the same type of dried grass that makes up the roof. More of it is piled near the door and the Q'ero spread it out as needed. Utilitarian objects such as woolen ropes hang from the pole rafters along with strips of dried meat, alpaca skins, and a collection of bones.

The children, their black hair messy and sticking up in every direction, peer at me from the blankets. Until they are six to eight years old, they go about completely unkempt. Other than at the time of the hair-cutting ceremony, which usually occurs around their first or second birthday, their hair is never combed, giving them the appearance of little wild men. Though sleepy eyed, they are the first to rise after the women and the hungriest. As soon as they have eaten, they whirl into nonstop activity, settling down only after nightfall when they eat ravenously and fall immediately asleep. In my 35 years of travel, much of it spent living with indigenous people, I have never seen as much energy as these children show. Their health is excellent. Other than injuries, skin rashes, and head lice, which have to be picked out daily by hand, making them appear like a troupe of forest primates as they comb through each other's hair with their fingers, Sebastian tells me that they are rarely sick.

It is another two hours before the sun rises over the hills and warms the air enough for me to venture outside. The frost disappears rapidly under the intense sun. The village has a clear view of the valleys below, as it is situated on high ground with only one way in. No one can approach without first being seen from a considerable distance. In that way, it is more like an encampment prepared for war, or escape, than a pastoral village.

The village is rimmed from behind on three sides by high mountains, and behind them by even higher ones. A stream fed from a lake at the base of one of those mountains tumbles past the village. Ten identical huts form a semicircle around a spring that is the principal water source, which the Q'ero tell me turns into a pond during the rainy season.

Esparilla, as the village is called, is part of another slightly larger one, Marcachaya, about an hour and a half walk farther down the valley. Another six villages are scattered throughout Q'ero territory, with the main one, Hatun Q'ero, a day's walk from here.

After a breakfast of potatoes, Sebastian delegates the day's responsibilities to each family member. Then, as we stand outside the hut warming ourselves in the sun, he points out the surrounding mountains, naming each as if they are old friends.

"This is Willaqoya. The next is Waranmanipa. The tallest is Apu Wayrumi. There is a lake up there and in a few days we will go there to do a *karpay*."

A *karpay* is a ceremony performed as part of a shaman's initiation and for special occasions. It can involve several *paqos* and community leaders, and is more complex than a *despacho*. My initiation in Q'ero is not only the culmination of years of working with Sebastian and Jorge, but the culmination of a lifetime of experiences with Native Americans and a considerable amount of time spent alone in wilderness areas. After years of experiences and some learning, it is about time that I display some knowledge. Later I understand, however, that the *karpay* doesn't mark the end, but the beginning of another phase of my training.

The second principle of the Andean way is called *yachay*. It means to learn, to know, and to remember. For the Q'ero, to learn and master the lifestyle required to live above 14,000 feet is essential for survival. To do this, they have to remember and learn from the experiences of others. It is then their responsibility to pass on what they have learned to future generations.

Yachay also implies the knowledge of things. The Q'ero have to know about healing plants, how to cultivate the soil, care for llamas and alpacas, and many other skills like weaving. The Incas were master stoneworkers, architects, and astronomers. They built extensive networks of roads, constructed elaborate temples in remote and inaccessible places, and worked gold and silver, ceramics, and fabric to a degree unequalled in the New World. The Q'ero inherited much of this knowledge.

They realize, however, that they also need to be flexible in their thoughts and actions. In an environment where wrong decisions can cause serious injury or sudden death, one has to be practical and recognize that it is necessary to apply what one learns in ways that work in the real world. Above all else, survival skills are the prerequisite for living in the Andes. Once the skills for maintaining life are mastered, however, the Q'ero take time for other things like dancing, art, and celebration.

True knowledge, the Q'ero believe, comes from direct personal experience guided by insight and intuition.

For the Andean shaman, knowledge is shaped by a lifetime of initiatory rites and isolation in wild nature. They are required to spend time alone often in caves, on the mountains, or in the forest. In some cases, it involves taking entheogens under the guidance of a master shaman.

It is a time-intensive process that won't be rushed. Shamans tend to provide information in pieces, randomly, not incrementally in an organized fashion, as in a school. These apparent fragments, endlessly repeated, make up the whole of a shaman's experience and, in many cases, the experiences of generations, forming a record of shamanic practices. The oral tradition is still the primary means by which knowledge and meaning are passed from one generation of shamans to the next.

My own learning about shamanism has taken half a lifetime. I've learned slowly, but over the years I have been able to put my own ideas out of the way and let the message of the Andean shamans penetrate me. Making the difficult journey to Q'ero was an essential part of the process.

There are different ways to learn. One of them is to study. First, study what others claim to know and, second, study directly from nature. Q'ero *paqos* practice both ways. They listen to the oral traditions transmitted by older *paqos* and also learn through direct interaction with nature. The other way to learn is to absorb and copy behavior, much as children do. This way of learning requires no thinking and is experiential; much of shamanic training happens in this manner in an apprenticeship under a master shaman.

The Q'ero exercise both ways of learning. They display a remarkable intelligence about their environment. Not only has every hill and mountain a name, but as we walk across the land, they teach me that every plant, each type of grass, bird, and animal has a name and use. The different types of rain, the kinds of frost and ice, and cloud formations all have names. The stars and constellations are known to them and, as Jorge later points out to me as we stand under a perfectly clear night sky, at one time the constellations were the "clock of the Incas."

When I put aside all my years of reading metaphysical books, I realize it is very simple. To practice the first principle, *munay,* you have to clear your heart and heal all the wounds buried there. To practice the second principle, *yachay,* you have to let go of opinions, judgmental behavior, and the idea that accumulation of information produces knowledge. In fact, too much information, even if supported by facts, often leads to confusion or, worse, dogmatism. Knowledge is acquired through carefully sifting through the facts and rearranging information to form a mental map that is true and useful. Knowledge does not have to be defended. This lessens the likelihood of conflicting opinions and the consequences of disagreement. *Munay,* as Sebastian told me, cannot exist when the mind is conflicted. So *yachay* also implies unlearning.

In the following days and between his duties and responsibilities, in our discussions but mostly by his example, Sebastian teaches me the ways of the Q'ero. He is assisted in this respect by the entire family, each member showing me different aspects of their world.

After several days in the village and when the moon is near full, Sebastian announces that the next day at noon we will perform the *karpay.* That morning, everyone rests, except for attending to duties like cooking and guarding the animals. Around ten, they adorn themselves with ceremonial attire. The older children wash in the spring and dress in miniature replicas of the adult outfits. The men wear brightly colored ceremonial ponchos and *ch'ullus,* the women and girls layers of black skirts hemmed in red with woven shawls of deep reds with geometric designs. They go bareheaded, with their hair in long braids, though some wear the same type of felt hat worn by men.

When all is ready, we proceed up the hill and into the mountains. The village recedes into the distance, becoming smaller and smaller until it vanishes from view. We walk along a stream with pools deep enough to bathe in. Trout dart in the shadows. Following it farther upstream, we come to where two streams converge. In the middle of the two waterways is a grassy island and we cross the shallow water to reach it.

Sebastian prepares for the cleansing ritual, the first part of the *karpay*. He instructs me to remove my jacket and down vest, take off my shoes and socks, and roll up my pant legs and sleeves. He grinds white quartz into powder in a mortar and adds herbs. He puts the mixture into a wooden cup and fills it with water.

"First, I will cleanse your body with water, plants, and the white rock of Q'ero," he says.

Then he bathes my arms and hands, legs and feet, and head with the medicinal water. The remainder he throws into the stream to be washed away.

"Next, I will cleanse your energy with herbs and flowers."

He takes a bundle of fresh plants he had brought along and rubs them over my entire body, followed by lightly brushing my arms, legs, chest, and back with his hands.

"Lastly, I will cleanse your deeper energy with an egg. It will draw out any residue of negative energy in your body, especially your heart."

He produces a fresh chicken egg and gently strokes my chest with it. When finished, he cracks it into the cup. Sebastian's wife, Phillipa, and Lorenzo look at it for signs of negative energy such as discoloration or deformity. Apparently there is none, as they sigh in relief. Then Sebastian throws the egg along with the remains of the herbs into the stream.

Cleansing in this manner is commonly employed among both North and South American Indians. Numerous ways to cleanse the body, mind, and energy are used, including sweat baths, bathing with plants and herbs, floral waters, and steam from natural hot springs. A cleansing ritual (*una limpieza* in Spanish) helps remove unseen obstacles that prevent one from functioning at the highest level. Ultimately, it clears away dark, malignant energy that hinders you from seeing reality—the oneness of all things.

Medicine men, shamans, and *curanderos* claim to see a web of living energy around a person's body. They can look into the body as well and see energy patterns in the person's organs and blood. When healthy, these patterns look like light or bright colors, such as blues, yellows, and greens. But when there is illness, these are seen as dark spots. In Quechua, beneficial, refined energy is called *sami* and is associated with good luck and health. During a *despacho,* the *paqo* exchanges his energy with that more refined energy of the *Apus* and then projects *sami* to the participants. One who receives beneficial energy is called a *samiyoq.* When you want to wish someone good luck, it is customary to say, *"Saminchay."* The opposite of *sami* is *hucha.* It is dark and malignant, contributes to bad luck and frequent mishaps, and is associated with faults and incorrect words or behavior. It needs to be cleansed away.

To accomplish this cleansing, North American medicine people burn sage or sweet grass in an abalone or other kind of seashell and fan the smoke with eagle feathers or those of other birds such as hawks considered to have strong "medicine" or energy. The Chumash of coastal California use the white wing feathers of seagulls or pelicans, believing that the white color signifies purity since these birds keep the beach clean. The shoreline, the transition place between water and land, is the optimal place for cleansing, they believe.

Mexican *curanderos* use the leafy branches of trees such as *pirule,* the California pepper tree, along with bundles of herbs and flowers such as purple Mexican sage and wild marigolds. In Oaxaca, in southern Mexico, aromatic resins like copal are often burnt in a clay vessel and one inhales the smoke to be purified.

Healers in the Amazon use bundles of fresh green plants

and herbs such as basil, fans made from dried palm leaves, and tobacco smoke. They also use floral baths and floral-scented waters. In the Amazon, drinking herbal medicines, ayahuasca, and resins from specific forest trees cleanses the body from the inside.

After the cleansing, we continue uphill until we come to a large rock. Though it contains only a shallow cave, I recognize it as a *waka*, a place where the spirits dwell. Sebastian stops and chooses a grassy spot on the side of the rock facing the mountain. He spreads his ceremonial objects on the ground and we sit in a semicircle in front of him. He pours out a large amount of coca leaves on a brightly colored cloth. The adults select *k'intus*, which they offer to another person. The act of offering coca in this manner symbolizes the principle of *ayni*, reciprocity. The best leaves are placed aside and kept for the ceremony.

When he has a sufficient number of *k'intus* and everyone is satiated, Sebastian puts the rest of the coca leaves away and spreads one of his deep red ceremonial cloths on the ground. Next he organizes each component of the *despacho* with great care. Lorenzo assists him. I sit to Sebastian's right and help prepare the offerings. The other Q'ero chew coca.

"In a *karpay*, each element must be in perfect order," he begins. "We use many of the same elements as in a regular *despacho*, but here there are additional ones of great importance."

Condor feathers are one of the special elements, and Sebastian takes out a bag of these and selects the best. He sets aside some of these for me to take home. Then he spreads a large sheet of colored paper over the ceremonial cloth. Usually, white paper is used, but he explains that for a *karpay* bright paper is better because it informs the *Apus* of the importance the *paqo* places on the ceremony.

"In the center, I place white cotton. It symbolizes clouds and they represent the upper world, *Hananpacha*," he says.

On top of the cotton, he places alpaca fat, quartz, and the condor feathers. In the center of these, he puts other objects, darker in color, including a llama fetus. "These are for the spirits of the lower world, *Ukhupacha.*"

Around them he places the elements of this world, *Kaypacha.* First he puts colored yarn and ribbons symbolizing rainbows, then elements appropriate to the female and male aspects of this world: silver on the left and gold on the right. Many other elements are added and when complete, he sprinkles confetti symbolizing stars and rain over everything.

He constructs a representation of the Incan cosmic vision. It includes *Pachamama* and *Inti,* the Sun, along with rain, rainbows, stars, and lightning. The main animals of the Andes are represented including llamas, alpacas, and condors. The array embraces the three levels of existence with specific offerings for the spirits of each. To finish, he adds the many *k'intus,* folds the paper by overlapping the four corners, and then wraps the entire package in the ceremonial cloth. In its folds, he tucks his personal shamanic objects, including a rattle and a large piece of white quartz.

Sebastian's wife starts a fire with dry grass in a hollow stone, then sprinkles aromatic resin on the coals. A sweet smell rises in the thin air. The smoke carries the intent of the ceremony to the *Apus* and the incense pleases the *Awkikuna.*

Next, Sebastian takes another *k'intu* and, kneeling, performs the *phuku* invoking *Pachamama* and the *Awkikuna.* Then he calls upon the *Apus,* naming each one.

"I send to you *Wiraqocha Santiago,*" he prays in Quechua. "Receive him as your son. Protect him. Guide his training and be with him on his journey."

I am deeply touched. Kneeling beside me, he hands me a *k'intu* and I perform the *phuku.* I pray that I be worthy of his trust in me, that I have the physical endurance to continue along the shamanic path, that my heart be open and mind clear, and that one day I come to live the mysteries of life with acceptance. Then I pray aloud as I hold the *k'intu* up to the *Apus:*

> *In your gentleness, I come.*
> *In your awesome power, I walk.*
> *In beauty, I find my way.*

The *Apus* must be listening. Insights pour into my mind and I realize the importance of having a clear heart and a free mind. Intellectual understanding is not enough to walk the shaman's path and practice the Andean principles. Emotional openness is limited. To be complete, the two must become harmonious. The integration of heart and mind fosters heart-centered consciousness. When lovingkindness is expressed in how we live and we have learned directly what life has to teach us, others see us as tranquil and harmonious. This is not something one obtains. Ironically, attaining it requires forgetting about how to get it. Once you have it, it cannot be taught. You can only live it. When this way of being is etched into the soul, one travels the inner roads of deep awareness in all aspects of daily life.

"*Munaycha,*" I say.

"*Hai!*" they exclaim in agreement. It is indeed a beautiful day.

While I am still kneeling, Sebastian passes the bundle over my body several times. He chants in Quechua and his voice carries on the wind and echoes off the mountain walls.

Carrying the ceremonial bundle, we proceed farther up the mountain. After walking some distance, we come to the base of the mountain that guards the back entry to Esparilla. It is a solid rock pinnacle without any vegetation. Caves are visible about halfway up one side.

"The next time you come, we will go up there to perform ceremonies. You'll see," Sebastian says, "it's a place of great power."

A small lake, the source of the water for the village, is located near the mountain's base. We stop there and Sebastian selects a place near the edge to complete the ceremony.

Lorenzo presents me with a *ch'ullu*. I had carried my poncho, but now put it on and remove my hat and replace it with the Q'ero cap. Everyone nods and smiles in approval.

Sebastian begins with an extensive prayer. He invokes every *Apu* in the mountain range. Then he raises the ceremonial bundle to the sky and blows into it seven times, prays again, blows five more times, and prays again. Then he asks me to kneel and, when I do, he places the bundle on my head. His concentration is one-pointed and holding the bundle to my head, he chants. Then we are finished.

The children gather dry grass and pile it high. Sebastian starts a fire. It ignites immediately and the smoke rises straight to the heavens. All comment on how auspicious it is. He throws the paper and its contents onto the fire and the bundle is immediately ablaze. Within minutes, it is consumed completely by the fire. In whispers, the Q'ero comment how powerful the energy is and how readily the spirits accepted the offerings.

The sun is well past its zenith when we finish. Sebastian has left some of his things at the *waka,* so we walk there to gather them before returning to the village. In the far distance, heavy mist is crawling up the valley and hiding the hills as it advances. We are higher and so above the mist and the Andean sun still shines intensely, but already the air is noticeably colder. By my observation, the only comfortable time of day in the winter season is between eleven in the morning and one in the afternoon.

"Alto kallpa," Sebastian says enthusiastically in a mixture of Spanish and Quechua, commenting on the ceremonial work as we arrive at the rock: "High energy!"

While Lorenzo and Sebastian's sons clean the area and gather up remaining items, he motions me to sit next to him on the poncho. The children and women head back to the village and Lorenzo goes off to tend to the horses. When we are alone, Sebastian opens his sacred bundle and takes out two stones.

"These are *kawsay qoyllu*," he said. "Healing stones."

I recognize the word for "life," *kawsay*, and know the general word for rocks and stones in Quechua is *rumi*. The other word, *qoyllu*, means to be energized by solar rays. I take this to mean these are life-giving stones used in shamanic work. One of them is almost black, the other a deep red; both are round, just larger than a golf ball.

"*Yanantin*," Sebastian says, using the word for a "sacred pair." "The darker one is the male and the lighter one the female."

He rubs them together. Then he takes the wooden cup that we used earlier in the cleansing ceremony by the stream. Phillipa filled it with water and left it for us. When a small amount of powder appears on the surface of the stones, he adds a little water and rubs them some more.

"This is how you make medicine from these," he tells me. "Rub them together until the blood of the stone comes out. When mixed in water, it strengthens the body."

Then he drops the liquid residue from rubbing the stones into the water in the wooden cup, drinks some of it, and passes it to me. I drink a little as well. It has a chalky taste, but is otherwise palatable. He pours some on the ground as an offering and finishes the rest.

"Q'ero *paqos* still heal in the ancient way using stones and plants. It's all about the magic of stones," Sebastian says.

The Incas were people of the stone and the greatest stonemasters of any civilization. Not only did they move huge boulders over great distances, but cut them into geometric shapes and with them constructed monuments and buildings with such precision that to this day a razor blade cannot pass through the joints. Stones were used for calendars, as shrines, and for healing.

For healing purposes, the Incas used several different types of stones. Some are shaped as llamas or mountain peaks and the points, symbolizing the *Apus,* are used to stimulate pressure points on the body (a kind of Andean acupressure). Others are round or circular and flat. These are placed on energy centers such as the solar plexus to rejuvenate the body's energy. Other types are heated and placed on sore muscles to help drive away cold that has penetrated the tissues, loosen contractions, and alleviate pain.

"The energy of the *Apus* and *Pachamama* is contained in these stones. Keep these with you at all times. They will protect you from accidental harm and ward off sorcery. They are part of the shaman's tools."

In the Andes, it's about stones. Incan stones, mountains, caves, and healing stones. Sebastian has told me of stone keys that opened portals in the rocks that lead to other dimensions, and about caves, their entrances long buried, that lead deep underground, including labyrinths under Sacsayhuaman and Cuzco. I have in my possession many healing stones.

Then Sebastian takes from his *ch'uspa* a metallic sphere about half the size of a golf ball. He hands it to me. It is unusually heavy for its size. I turn it over in my palm. It's carved with what at first looks like a fish. On closer inspection, it could be a spaceship.

"Where did this come from?" I ask.

"We find these," he says.

"Who carved the design?"

"*Nadia.* No one. They come this way."

"Are they exactly like this when you find them?"

"*Sí,* exactly. They fall from the sky."

I am surprised. More mysteries in the Andes. How could round metal balls etched with what appears to be a spacecraft fall from the sky? During the *karpay,* I was presented to the *Apus.* I was cleansed in different stages as we ascended the

mountain, preparing for the initiation. Now, after the ceremony, it is as if I am worthy in his eyes to see more.

"These have *hatun kallpa*, high energy. When the time is
right, you will find one," Sebastian says, this time using the
Quechua word instead of *alto*.

Sebastian prays to the *Apus* of Q'ero during the *karpay*.

Author and Sebastian in common everyday ponchos

The Way of Action

The way of action is the third principle of Q'ero life. It is called *llank'ay* (pronounced yan-kay). The literal translation means "to work." The spirit of *llank'ay*, however, goes beyond physical labor and includes mental and creative work, as well as performing ceremonies and healing. Ceremonial life imbues work with meaning and, to the Q'ero, balancing outer activity with inner work is the key to survival. Ceremonial work is not isolated from physical work. The planted field is holy ground just like the mountains.

Though each of the first three principles is a separate element with its own characteristics, they are synergistic. The three work as a whole, interdependent and mutually supportive. For example, love and beauty, *munay*, make daily life pleasing and soften the hard edges of difficulty. Also, without initiating right action, *llank'ay*, nothing gets done and things stagnate. Action for its own sake can lead to conflict, however. The best outcome of actions proceeds from knowledge, *yachay*, the second principle.

As one learns and grows, each principle transforms into a higher form. *Munay* becomes impersonal love that embraces all things. *Yachay* becomes the superior consciousness one arrives at through the proper cultivation of love and work. *Llank'ay* is not just work and routine ritual, but becomes right livelihood. A way of living that is ecologically sound, promotes the welfare of others, and encourages service performed in the spirit of lovingkindness is central to the higher form of *llank'ay*.

Another way to think about these fundamental principles is, as I have noted previously, that they consist of the ability to feel, think, and act. Just to work, or just to think, or to be consumed by one's emotions is imbalanced and antithetical to the Andean way. When in harmony, these principles balance an individual. According to Andean belief, for one to be at peace and happy, it is necessary to harmonize these in one's manner and daily life. Only when the emotions, thoughts, and actions are aligned can you be a balanced human.

Prior to my coming to Q'ero, I was possessed by a desire to be up to the physical challenge of a trip into the high Andes. But the altitude, cold, and my injured feet thwart my hopes of climbing into the mountains that surround the village and they nearly cripple me. The result is to make me idle when I crave activity and preoccupied with my ailments when I want more time for spiritual insight. I try not to lose sight of my purpose, but it becomes nearly impossible to maintain composure in the midst of my foot pain and the debilitating effects of high altitude.

Though disappointed with myself, I take it as a lesson in the cultivation of right action. I refocus my attention on survival and not on my personal thoughts, opinions, and desires. I suppose I could do something like whittle, but there are no sticks to carve on. I might read, but I didn't bring a book. Instead, I write in my journal and observe the daily routines of village life.

The Q'ero are sympathetic to my plight and their concern is apparent, but they don't coddle me. Instead, they offer helpful suggestions on how I might heal faster and provide me with herbal remedies. It just takes time. They know that and make preparations for the day when I will recover.

My feet gradually heal, the altitude has less effect on me, and I learn to dress in a way that makes it easier to adapt to the hot midday sun and freezing temperature the rest of the time. When I am able to walk without significant pain, I go to the potato fields where my lesson in the third principle begins.

For the Q'ero, to work is to survive. They prepare the fields for planting, sow potatoes, harvest them, and repeat the cycle year after year, century upon century. Due to the extremes in weather and high altitude, however, each aspect of Andean agriculture requires meticulous planning and coordination in accord with seasonal changes.

Besides potato-growing, Q'ero lifestyle is pastoral. They tend llamas, alpacas, sheep, horses, a few cattle, and a pig or two. Domestic work for women includes cooking, spinning and weaving, and working in the fields beside their men. Child care, dish and clothes washing, and cooking are shared by men and women. Communal work called *faena* in Spanish is common among Andeans. Houses are raised in this manner and if a man is away or sick, his fields are worked by the others until his return.

For traditional Andeans, the cycle of work is ruled by astronomical events such as the solstices, as well as climatic occurrences such as the beginning and end of the rainy season. Potato planting is crucial. It is timed to the movement of the Pleiades across the heavens. A clear sky filled with bright stars and an unobstructed view of the Pleiades (*Vilcacoto* in Quechua) as they rise in the night sky is the best time to sow.

So it is early June now, potato harvest time, and just before the grand annual celebrations of *Q'lloryti* and *Inti Rami*. Every member of Sebastian's family is eager to get the potatoes out of the fields, dried, and bagged, so they can attend the celebrations. Having rested for several days, I feel better and, wanting to work with them in the *chakra,* offer to help.

The next morning, Sebastian and Lorenzo leave early to attend a meeting in Marcachaya, an hour and a half walk from their village.

They will not return until after dark. Around midmorning, I go with Rolando to the potato fields, also an hour and a half walk, but in a different direction.

We start when the sun has warmed the air sufficiently and we follow a llama trail along the side of hills covered by a sticky grass with a glossy resin. I brush against it and it sticks to my clothes and irritates my skin. Rolando warns me about it and in the future I avoid touching it. Banks of mist move in and out of the valley below us. We come upon a group of llamas loaded with potatoes packed in plastic sacks. It is harvest time. Other llamas with brown alpacas graze on the slopes above us. Far below runs a fast flowing stream with pools deep enough to dive into if the water weren't ice cold. Later, I learn that the Andean sun heats the surface of the water so much that, by eleven in the morning, it is warm enough to bathe in. Rolando tells me that the stream is full of trout and later proves it by bringing home a dozen firm-fleshed fish for dinner.

On the plateau overlooking the valley, we come upon an Incan ruin. It may have been a way station or house at one time, but is now just a cluster of stones. An ancient tree with tangled aboveground roots, the only tree in the entire area, has grown around the stones. The place feels haunted and Rolando avoids it, but I find it fascinating and approach the tree with an offering of coca leaves. Rolando, maintaining a respectful distance, observes me with interest, but doesn't come closer.

From the vantage point of the ruin, the valley and hills are visible for miles in every direction. Fields under cultivation form a patchwork quilt on the hillsides, black soil contrasted with pale brown grasses, which makes them visible from a distance. Rolando points out Sebastian's fields, still a long distance away, but clearly larger than the others around it. Later, I find out that Sebastian is responsible for feeding 30 people, and his sphere of responsibility extends indirectly to many more.

We walk away from the ruin and continue downhill along a draw until we come to the base of a large hill. Mountains rise up in all directions around us. At the base of the hill, black soil matted with grass roots, exposed by hand-turning with a crude tool akin to a wooden shovel, lies exposed to the sun. We make our way over the clods of dark earth up the hill to where several members of Sebastian's family are camped in a grass hut not much larger than a small tent. This is where they sleep and cook when working in the fields.

After a rest and lunch of boiled potato and egg soup, the work of harvesting potatoes continues. Once the potatoes swell in the ground, they are dug up by hand with crude, heavy metal hoes. The children gather the potatoes, still covered with a few soft clods of earth until they air dry. This laborious process is mostly completed, so our job is to gather the potatoes and carry them to the top of the hill where we lay them on dry grass. Here, they dry more and much of their dirt falls off. Afterward, they are packed into sacks for transportation back to the village.

Native to the Andes, there are 4,000 varieties of wild and cultivated potatoes. Most are frost-tolerant, an asset at high elevations where freezing temperatures occur in all seasons. Other tubers, similar to potatoes but from different botanical families, are also cultivated. One of these, the *moraya,* is the size of a large marble and as hard. It is processed by first sun-drying and then repeatedly freeze-drying the tubers by exposing them to the cold mountain air. Preparing them to eat is an ordeal. It involves cracking and pounding each one with a heavy stone and then grinding the pieces into a fine white powder to make a starchy but tasty and nourishing porridge called *ch'uñu.*

The Q'ero cultivate and eat a variety of potatoes and tubers, often in the same meal. All of these are small, the largest being not much fatter than one's thumb. Cooking facilities consist of an open fire where potatoes are boiled in metal pots. Communal meals are eaten three times daily. Sometimes they add alpaca meat, intestines or other parts, or small amounts of onions, but a typical meal consists of a large bowl of boiled potatoes followed by potato broth.

At first, I couldn't understand how they existed on a high-carbohydrate, low-protein, low-fat diet. Potatoes contain, however, a wide range of vitamins and minerals, especially when grown on nutrient rich soil, as in the Andes. When combined with other tuberous roots that are higher in protein, such as the *moraya,* they provide a balanced if monotonous diet. The addition of alpaca meat, an occasional egg, and trout adds variety and protein. The high-carbohydrate content of their diet provides energy to work and walk long distances in the Andes. Judging by their strength, endurance, and the perfect shape of their teeth, the Q'ero are in excellent health and their traditional diet suits them.

In my first days in Q'ero, altitude sickness robbed me of my appetite and strength. Though the Q'ero encouraged me to eat more and keep hydrated by drinking copious quantities of potato broth, I simply had no appetite to do so. They rarely drink water, believing that cold water robs the body's energy and makes one intolerant to the extremes in weather in the high Andes. They do, however, drink lots of broth, and sometimes drink tea made from wild herbs or coca leaves. I was able to drink several cups of coca leaf tea (*mate de coca*) daily, which helped restore my strength and appetite.

By the time I get to the fields, my appetite has returned. I am not sufficiently strong to work alongside them for long, however. This proves embarrassing for me. Generally, I have abundant energy and, since I grew up on a farm in New England, I am accustomed to the toil and joy of physical labor. Here with the Q'ero, I work as long as I can, but by the afternoon I have to stop and rest on the grass.

The Q'ero approach work with great care. In the field, they treat each potato with importance and cover it with dry grass. They take their work seriously and mostly work in silence, but break into light conversation readily. Smiles flash at every opportunity. Small children and dogs play among the workers, and the children are encouraged to find any remaining tiny potatoes that escaped the eyes of the adults.

After several days of this, I spend time in the village observing the next stage. After the potatoes are collected and dried, they are bagged and hauled to the village on llamas. Once in the village, each sack is emptied and the potatoes sorted for size and type. Spoiled ones are set aside for the animals to eat. Between his many other duties, Lorenzo does most of this work. He is tireless and, though he is very busy, I find him attentive to my questions. He shows me which potatoes to save as seed for the following season and how to choose among the piles those that are unfit for eating due to deformity or ones that are too small. He also chooses some that appear unusually robust, which he considers will make for continued generations of healthy potatoes, and puts those with the seed potatoes.

In the late afternoon, the women begin cooking. Lorenzo works with them, often doing much of the food preparation and cooking. From his experience as a porter and assistant cook on the Inca Trail, he learned different culinary skills, such as using instant soup stock to flavor the otherwise bland potato broth.

The Q'ero work cooperatively and harmoniously. They learn from early childhood that survival requires work and cooperation. Never have I seen a show of dominance by one individual over another and, though the work ethic is strong, it is not overbearing. The intensity of the work demands commitment.

For those among the group who aren't up to the demands of the work, criticism comes indirectly. Rolando, for example, receives his share of disapproval in a well-aimed but carefully worded sentence or two when he loses his attention. He prefers fishing to fieldwork and, since he is a good fisherman, he's often given permission to take his net to the river. Here he fishes for trout and always comes home with at least a dozen.

The Q'ero understand that each person has a unique gift. Some are better suited to tending llamas and alpacas in the heights, often sleeping for days or weeks at a time in makeshift huts of dry grass or in caves. To keep themselves company, they play flutes made of bone. The ethereal sound they make is heard across valleys and over mountains. Llamas are capable of caring for themselves but must be guarded against attack and from being eaten by pumas and foxes, or by condors during the birthing season.

Others, like Lorenzo, have multiple abilities. During my stay in Q'ero, I observe that he is equally at home cooking as butchering and skinning an alpaca or working the fields. A rare few, like Rolando, are called to spend time alone in the mountains. First, as young children they are drawn to the rocks and streams where nature spirits dwell. Later, they venture farther into the hills and eventually into the most remote snow-covered peaks. These individuals become shamans.

In Quechua, as I previously mentioned, a shaman is called *paqo,* which is the same word for a male alpaca, a shorter and stockier version of the llama, but with longer hair prized for its wool. Alpacas can live at high altitudes in extreme weather, existing on small amounts of sparse grass and herbs, and are content to sleep under the stars. So too the Andean shaman spends time in the high mountains subsisting on wild herbs and coca leaves. Such experiences foster the development of wisdom and other traits of an Andean shaman-priest.

Though supported by their family and community during periods of training, a *paqo* is not exempt from working in the potato field or from other duties. In fact, the shaman's work is twice as hard. They marry, have children, and raise families like other members of the community. In addition to routine chores, however, they conduct ceremonies of reciprocity.

The Q'ero have an organized system by which they live that includes routine work as well as ceremonies and celebrations. It requires detailed knowledge of the environment and attunement with seasonal changes. They appear to me to be happy even though they take their duties seriously and purposefully. They are never too busy or serious, however, to acknowledge the natural beauty around them. In this manner, the circle of life for them is complete.

Q'ero textile used in ceremonies; designs represent Inti, the Sun.

Close-up of Q'ero textile; design represents the four corners of the Incan empire of the Sun, *Tawantinsuyu*.

The Way of Life

The fourth Q'ero principle is *kawsay* and means "life." This doesn't encompass its real meaning, however. *Kawsay* refers to the matrix of energy or the web of life that links all living things on Earth. In that way, it is connected to *Pachamama*. Earth-time and life are inseparable. Therefore, *Pachamama* is not only the ground on which we live and that supports all things, but it is also imbued with life-giving energy. The Q'ero call this intertwining of life and energy *kawsay pacha,* the world of living energy.

From the Andean view, to live harmoniously, it is necessary to balance the human sphere and environmental forces. This is accomplished through attunement with the world of living energy. *Pachamama* is permeated with this living energy, so all life is sacred, and therefore ceremonies play a significant role in maintaining this attunement. The way we live is as important, however, as how we ceremonially interact with the forces of life. Balance between daily life and ritual is maintained through reciprocity (called *ayni,* discussed in the next chapter), the interchange of energy through works, deeds, actions, thoughts, emotions, and things. In this way, all five principles work synergistically and complete the circle of life.

Earlier, I explained that, to the Q'ero, all natural things are material yet possess an innate intelligence. Peruvians who abide by this teaching refer to this intelligence as a "mother" or *madre*. Ayahuasca shamans claim to "see" these *madre* spirits as luminous beings. Lightning, thunder, animals, trees, rocks, birds, insects, mountains, lakes, rivers, rainbows, earthquakes, hail, snow, ice, and rain compose the Andean landscape. Each has a luminous counterpart that can communicate with humans in an intuitive way. The force that infuses them is *kallpa*.

This worldview is not too different from the Santiago theory of cognition, first proposed by the British anthropologist Gregory Bateson in 1973, elaborated on by Humberto Maturana of the University of Chile in Santiago, and popularized by Fritjof Capra in *The Web of Life*. The central insight of the Santiago theory is that the process of knowing is inseparable from the process of life. Summarized in his *The Tree of Knowledge*, Dr. Maturana proposed that "living systems are inferential, inductive, cognitive, circular, and historical." Life is relationships.

Sebastian taught me that the *Apus* are not just mountains to be respected as natural temples, but also powerful spiritual beings that communicate and influence the destiny of men. For the Q'ero, it is not incongruent for coca leaves to speak and for stones to heal. For me, this meant that I needed to suspend my Western material, judgmental thinking, even if I didn't fully embrace Andean beliefs, in order for the Q'ero to trust that I would respect what they told me.

The *Awkikuna* that populate the landscape are magical beings who manipulate *kallpa* in positive or negative ways. They use it to maintain the natural order of things by helping crops and animals, influencing the weather, and guarding rivers. They rarely interact directly with humans. They can also cause illness if offended or disrespected. Shamans develop similar abilities during their training. The currency that *paqos* use to interact with the world of spirits is *kallpa*. They use this energy for healing, to change one's luck, ward off evil, and alter destiny.

Not only do natural things like mountains, trees, and stones have *kallpa*, but thoughts and feelings also have it. These can be positive or negative in form and outcome, and heavy or light in character.

Hucha darkens mood, decreases resistance to disease, and causes sluggishness and poor health. It can be lightened by natural beauty like colorful flowers, or burning sweet-smelling resins or *palo santo* (dried wood of the *Burserea graveolens* tree). Herbal and floral baths are commonly employed in Peru for this purpose. Prayers, chanting, and drumming are traditional ways of regulating energy and restoring balance. Andeans consider rainbows auspicious. Rainbows are represented symbolically in *despachos* by colored ribbon or threads and used for their potent healing powers to lighten the burden of heavy energy.

Sometimes, energy may be too light and needs balancing and grounding. For this, the Incas used healing stones shaped as animals, such as llamas, or as mountain peaks symbolizing the *Apus*. Each stone has one or more pointed edges to stimulate pressure points on the patient's body, similar to acupuncture. Some stones are round and without points, composed of iron and other minerals that make them very heavy; they are used to help ground people who are disconnected from physical reality. When placed on different parts of the body, the stones help restore energy and strengthen the body. They remove stagnant and blocked energy, making the person feel lighter.

My ethnomedical research in Peru and Mexico has convinced me that there is more to healing than pharmaceutical drugs, psychotherapy, or even natural medicines when used in an allopathic way. Shamanic healing reestablishes resonance among the body's biological systems and restores its inherent energetic state—a tune-up of homeostasis. When harmony is restored to the world of living energy within us by balancing heavy and light energy, healing takes place. In this sense, shamans and *curanderos* are better "healers" than doctors who provide only a treatment prescribed from on high by a drug company or health organization.

In healing, the Andean shaman-priest regulates, harmonizes, and transforms *kallpa,* the life force. He does this with herbal medicines (*hanpi* in Quechua), healing stones, feathers, offerings of coca leaves, and other ritual things, especially sweets, pleasing to the *Apus, Awkikuna,* and *Pachamama.* A master shaman, the *altomesayoq,* can heal and alter a person's destiny through his presence alone. Since there are few such highly developed individuals, ceremonies are required to make the desired changes. Second best, but helpful when performed by a skilled shaman.

A typical session starts by creating a sacred space. Andean shamans do this by selecting a suitable place, preferably in nature where the *Awkikuna* reside, such as caves, a grove of trees, or an unusual rock formation. When working in someone's home, they lay their sacred objects on their ceremonial cloth to form a *mesa* and burn fragrant resins. Amazonian shamans use tobacco smoke from *mapacho* and may also use aromatic plants and flowers. Next, through focused concentration, the shaman clears his consciousness from unwanted influences, thoughts, memories, and desires. He may also establish a rhythm by shaking a rattle or beating a drum to assist the participants to remain calm and focused.

Once a sacred space is established, the Q'ero shaman-priest summons the most powerful spirits at his disposal, the *Apus.* A *despacho* may also be performed. This serves several purposes. First, as an act of reciprocity, it acknowledges the help of the spirits. Second, it directs healing energy from the spiritual realms through the healer to the recipient. Third, it serves to cleanse the sick individual of *hucha,* bad luck *(malo suerte),* and evil influences. Fourth, it forms a link between the individual and the soul that may have wandered off, as in cases of *el susto*.

Next, the shaman-priest diagnoses the cause and location of the illness or *malo suerte*. Causes may be natural such as accidents, bad winds, or excessive cold or heat. Illness may also be caused, however, by fright, envy, malicious intent by another person, one's own bad thoughts, or, worse, sorcery. The latter is by far the most serious of causes and is dealt with using great care and attention. In cases of sorcery, the shaman's own well-being is vulnerable to attack.

Treatment involves chanting, rattles or other percussive instruments, and burning aromatic resins. I think of this as modulating the energy field of the recipient. The shaman-priest attempts to restore balance and harmony within the individual and between the individual and his family and village and the natural environment, including the world of spirits. Heavy, dark, distorted energy in the ill person is cleansed and realigned, beautified. Herbal treatments including teas, poultices, and plasters, and the use of stones, massage, and baths may be employed. Rituals may be prescribed, such as making an offering to a specific *Apu*, burying ritual objects, or the offering of *chicha* (the fermented corn beer called *aqha* in Quechua) or other liquids of ritual importance, such as llama's blood. Special diets are often recommended, as is sexual abstinence.

It is late afternoon. The sun is warm and the family is outside enjoying the warmth. The women wash their hair in the stream while the children play in the cold water. Their few scrawny yellow dogs skirmish over the scarps. Lorenzo and Guillermo wash their ponchos and then spread them on the roof of the hut to dry. Cream-colored llamas graze the steep hillside opposite the village. I am amazed that they are so sure-footed that they never fall from even the steepest slopes.

Sebastian and I watch the activities. He wears his gray poncho, red and yellow *ch'ullu*, and the short, black, traditional Andean pants. This style of dress hasn't changed since the time of the Incas. One of his sandal straps has broken loose. He takes off his poncho and, sitting on it, begins to work the pieces until it is repaired. We sit without speaking for an hour. As the sun sets, it illuminates the valley and hills.

"The world is changing," Sebastian says. "Once, we lived here isolated from everything, but we were content and happy. There was no sickness. We treated minor ailments with plants. We are still removed from everything, but the world has found us. It is closing in and we have nowhere else to go."

He is right. Chemical pollutants are found in the Arctic, so why not here? Global warming is changing climates. Increasing population is using up natural resources at an alarming rate. The Q'ero have held out for four hundred years, but they cannot hold on while global conditions erode the environment on which they depend. For the immediate future, they can survive. In 15 or so years, they may be unable to.

I look at him closely. He keeps his hair short so it falls forward. His feet are calloused and wide, his calves muscular. For his short stature, he is strong. In the mountains, he is indefatigable and capable of carrying tremendous loads on his back for days. In the Andes, Q'ero Indians, like the Sherpas of Nepal, are valued as porters for mountain climbers and tourists who walk the Inca Trail, though Sebastian has never worked this trade. There is wisdom in this man.

In our technological world, we tend to think that if things go wrong, a brilliant scientist will find a way to fix things. To me, this is counterintuitive. For ecological understanding, perhaps the scientists should consult the Q'ero and other traditional Indian people.

"*Pachamama* and the *Apus* are not respected," he says.

In the Andes, the greatest force of *kawsay* is found within *Pachamama* and the *Apus*. Of the two, the *Apus* are the more powerful and are the most important of all spiritual beings in the mystical world of the Incas. They manifest "male" energy, whereas *Pachamama* is "female." The *Apus* radiate light; their colors are white and sky blue. *Pachamama*'s colors are greens, rich browns, and deep blues. The energy of the Earth is nourishing and sustaining, fecund and fertile. At times, it can be destructive, however, as in earthquakes or floods. The energy of the *Apus* is remote, brilliant, so powerful that only the most adept shaman can control it.

I look for a medical reason for why the *Apus* are considered so powerful. Living at high altitudes not only requires physiological adaptation, but it also affects the brain and consciousness. At altitudes of 14,000 feet and higher, one may experience excessive nighttime wakefulness, unusual dreams, and even hallucinations. The Andean light is intensely brilliant, making the weird rock formations appear all the more otherworldly. I believe these factors may contribute to a state of mind that has driven saints and sages to seek the high mountains for inspiration and Andeans to worship their permanently snow-covered peaks.

"Santiago," Sebastian says, looking at me seriously, "Q'ero is still pure and the energy is good here. I am worried about the rest of the world."

"*Hai!*" I answer. "Yes. I agree."

"We are in a time of great change. My people have waited for hundreds of years for the return of the Inca. That time may be upon us."

The Incas believed the passing of time is composed of daily, monthly, seasonal, and annual cycles, but also of greater cycles. Each of these grand cycles lasts from eight hundred to one thousand years. According to them, the time between cycles, from the ending of one world to the beginning of the next, is marked by an overturning of Earth-time called a *pachakuteq*. Incan prophecy says that we are nearing the next one. What gives credibility to this prediction are similar prophecies from Buddhist, Aztec, Mayan, and Hopi traditions.

The Incas organized historical time into five ages, the fifth age being the time of the Incan Empire and still ongoing at the Conquest. According to Andean calculations, the era associated with the ascendancy of European world dominance ended between 1990 and 1993. In 1994, world events began to shift as Middle Eastern and Asian cultures challenged the West. We are now in a transitional period from 2000 to 2012. During this time, a cosmic restructuring will occur, setting the stage for *Inkari,* the return of the Inca, and a new golden era of spirituality and the restoration of the Earth's environment.

Talking about energy and prophecy makes me think again of the legend of Paititi, the lost city of the Incas, and of the hidden monastery supposed to be on the eastern slope of the Andes near the border of Peru and Bolivia, not far from Q'ero. I ask Sebastian about these. This time he is more willing to talk.

"Of course, we know about these places. Our elders tell us that this is not the time for them to be found. The shamans of old possessed magical stones, keys that unlocked the doors to other worlds."

"Do these magical stone keys still exist?"

"Yes, they do, but they are lost."

I can only imagine such things. For now, I am content to sit with Sebastian in the mountains.

Over time, I've learned that *kawsay* is not static but everchanging. Though the first three principles—*munay*, *yachay*, and *llank'ay*—are the foundation of the Andean way, *kawsay* is its prerequisite. Without being alive, we cannot experience or practice these principles.

"*Hatun kallpa,*" I exclaim.

"*Hai!*" he answers. "High energy."

Samples of ancient healing stones in the author's collection

A completed *despacho*

The Way of Reciprocity

Of the five principles, *ayni* is the single most important concept of the Andean way. It is translated as reciprocity and means the interchange of lovingkindness, knowledge, and the fruits of one's labor between individuals, between humans and the environment, and between humans and nature spirits. Reciprocity implies that one's labor is shared: I will help you today, and tomorrow you might help me. The purpose of reciprocity is the maintenance of life.

Ayni provides purpose for the first three principles. It makes them function, gives them structure, and holds them as the banks of a river contain the flow of water until it reaches the sea. In this way, *ayni* sustains and supports all of life, *kawsay*.

Ayni also implies respect for life. This is shown through acts of reciprocity. Respect is the key to understanding the Andean way. When we return the good that comes to us and show respect without judging the giver or what is received, it becomes benevolence in its highest form. In this way, *munay* and *anyi* are interconnected.

Ayni is the central code of the Q'ero and the root of Andean values. *Ayni* is deeper than mutual respect and helping others, however. It implies the conscious and willing acknowledgment of the interconnection between humans and the natural world that sustains them. Traditionally, this takes the form of ritual offerings to *Pachamama,* the *Apus, Awkikuna, Qhaqya* (the thunder god), and other nature spirits in the *despacho* ceremony.

To Andeans, the Earth is not just our world, but is shared by all things visible and invisible. Interchange between these is the work of the shaman-priest. The ceremonies that Andean *paqos* perform are symbolic acts of this type of reciprocity.

Sebastian explained it to me in this way: "When we offer respect through the *despacho,* it assures harmony in our community and the surrounding land. The spirits of the mountains, the streams, the rain, and *Pachamama* are pleased. Our newborn infants and baby animals are delivered easily and are born healthy, our fields yield abundantly, and the alpacas and llamas are strong and don't get sick."

Ayni includes shared beauty and not just beautiful things. When Sebastian comments on a remarkable Andean day or how nature synchronistically cooperates during a ceremony, he is sharing beauty with me. It is as if he is saying: "Let's look at this together. Let's share the beauty of this moment." Likewise, when you watch a glorious sunset with a friend, you are practicing *ayni.*

In the time of the Incas, reciprocity involved the ritual offering of things of beauty to the spirits. Gold, the most important metal of the Incas, is associated with the Sun (*Inti*), and figurines of llamas and other gold objects were offered to *Inti.* Objects made from gold were also placed in graves alongside mummies as offerings to beings in the spiritual world when the soul of the deceased person entered the place of the dead. Blood, considered the fluid of life, was the primary offering to

Pachamama. Aqha Mama, the spirit of the traditional Andean fermented corn drink, was an important offering. It symbolizes the vital fluid of plants. In modern times, gold foil or gold-colored paper is used in place of real gold, and blood sacrifices have been replaced with red wine, though in remote villages, llamas are still ritually sacrificed.

Respect and reciprocity are not exclusive to ceremonies, however. *Ayni* is also important in daily life. Andean people practice this principle in the organization of *faenas,* the communal work parties that since Incan times have built terraces and irrigation canals, and planted and harvested crops. To this day, work parties are a common sight in the Andes. After the day's work is done, the group often meets to play music and enjoy each other's company away from the fields and drink *aqha.*

To illustrate the practical aspect of reciprocity, Sebastian says, "If you plant only a few potatoes, you harvest only some. But if you prepare sufficient ground and plant lots of potatoes, you harvest more. If you have more potatoes, you can share the surplus with others. That's *ayni.*"

Ayni applies to animals and plants as well as humans and spirits. The most important Andean plant, coca, is treated with the utmost respect and is commonly referred to as *Mama Coca.* Before chewing coca leaves, a *k'intu* is made. When a group of people are chewing coca together, they offer each other *k'intus* as a ritual form of *ayni.* Before drinking water, *aqha,* or any alcohol, it is customary to pour a small amount on the ground as a symbolic offering to *Pachamama.*

Women are also treated respectfully. When speaking to a woman of any age, it is polite to address her as *Mamita,* little mother. To the Andean, all women are representatives of *Pachamama,* the great Earth Mother. They deserve our respect because they create new human life in their womb, and because they nourish and nurture.

To the Andean, the purpose of human life is to achieve and maintain balance between the human sphere and nature. To live harmoniously is to achieve inner peace. When you have inner peace, you are happy and healthy. *Ayni* may be exactly what the modern world needs.

In Q'ero, when a special bond of friendship develops between two people, they may chose to enter into a relationship that makes them spiritual kin. One example of this is the "hair-cutting ceremony." After a baby is born, its hair is left to grow naturally until it is ceremonially cut. During these occasions, the one who cuts the child's hair becomes a godmother *(comadre)* or godfather *(compadre)*. This manner of bonding requires deep respect and concern. It is a spiritual contract and is taken very seriously by the Q'ero.

I am fortunate and have become *compadre* to two baby girls in Sebastian's family. In this way, I am an extended family member and part of the Q'ero nation.

Several days after the *karpay*, we discuss a hair-cutting ceremony for Lorenzo's youngest daughter, Yenika. Even this discussion has an air of formality to it. We are sitting on the floor of the hut and Lorenzo approaches me with respect and asks if I would be willing to be his daughter's godfather, *compadre*. I agree, but at the time do not realize the importance placed on this ritual by the Q'ero. To them, the hair-cutting ceremony is a bond for life. Lorenzo is ecstatic. He dances around the hut, and his wife, usually very shy, smiles broadly and her dark eyes sparkle like sunlight upon water.

The morning of the hair-cutting ceremony, Lorenzo rises in the dark and heads into the mountains to find an alpaca to butcher. He returns around noon with the meat. He places the skin covered in thick white fur in the sun to dry. The women cut pieces of fresh alpaca meat and prepare potatoes and a special dish made from a freeze-dried tuber similar to a potato, called *ch'uñu*. They make this into a thick, rich-tasting, starchy porridge.

While the women prepare the food, Sebastian and I lounge in the warm sun like two lizards. He talks of how his people are connected to their history and land, and tells me about their relationship to the mountains. I listen, and we share the beauty of the day together.

On three sides surrounding the village are a series of mountains and, though he has told me their names several times before, he tells me again.

He names them one by one: "This is Apu Wayrumi. Next is Willaqoya. Here is Apu Siyacasa and then Salkanuyu. Between them is the way to Apu Ausangate. Far behind them is the sacred mountain of Q'ero, Apu Wamanlipa."

To our right are several large hills that he calls Colca. Below them is a stream that cuts through the rock to form deep circular pools. Beside it is the trail to Marcachaya, the sister village of Esparilla. Far to the south is a range of mountains that separate Q'ero from the rest of the Andes and isolate it from the world.

"We Q'ero live close to the *Apus*," he says. "They protect us, but they can also be dangerous. Their power is immense. Only *Inti*, the Sun, is more powerful. You have finally come to the land of the *Apus*. Tomorrow, we will journey across these mountains toward Apu Ausangate. It will take us several days. The passes are higher than those we crossed coming here. You will be tested not only in body but in spirit."

Our conversation is interrupted when Lorenzo appears in the doorway of the stone hut. Beaming from ear to ear, he tells us that it is time to eat. The entire family is present along with guests from a neighboring village. Plates of fried alpaca meat are passed around, followed by trout, alpaca intestines, and other delicacies. They have few plates, so each must be washed between courses and often several people eat from one bowl. The ubiquitous boiled potatoes appear and are followed by potato soup in a base of alpaca meat.

After we have eaten, they prepare for the hair-cutting. Sebastian's wife spreads a cloth on the ground and places on it a bowl covered with another cloth to catch the clippings. Every one gathers around. Lorenzo hands me a pair of cheap scissors. I examine them and wonder how I am going to use them as they seem dull. His wife carries their eight-month-old girl who cries and struggles like a wild animal to get free. She is so strong that it takes three adults to hold her still enough so I can cut her hair. Though she is younger than the usual age for hair cutting, one or two years old, I suspect they considered her big and strong enough.

I go to work as best I can and clip her head of black hair that looks as if it has never seen a comb. It is matted in every con- ceivable manner and sticks out in all directions. At first I try to cut it so it has at least a crude shape, but they encourage me to cut more. Following their instructions, I cut every strand of hair as close to the scalp as possible. By the time I finish, she is nearly bald. Lorenzo holds her up for everyone to admire. There is so much life force in her that she continues to struggle and kick to get free until he passes her to her mother and she starts nursing.

The cutting part over, there are still formalities to complete. Sebastian's wife cleans up the clippings and wraps them in the ceremonial cloth. Then each person in turn gives me a firm hug and calls me *compadre*.

Lorenzo stands and gives a short speech in Quechua; then, switching to Spanish, he says: "You are family now. With that goes the responsibility of treating this girl as your daughter. Will you honor this pact forever?"

Forever, I think, is a big word. What does forever mean to the Q'ero?

"I will."

Everyone is overjoyed.

Afterward, they dress me in traditional finery—a brightly

colored poncho, my new *ch'ullu,* a felt hat with an ornamental band made of white beads, and necklaces of the same white beads. We embrace again and then go outside to take pictures with my camera.

We rest in the afternoon. I walk up the hill behind the village and relax by the stream. Mountains surround me and grassy hills roll across the landscape for miles in front of me. I watch the sun set behind the mountains and the hills turn golden. Mist and low clouds move rapidly from below and shroud the village.

Dinner is the same soup but with alpaca intestines in the potato broth, boiled potatoes, and large portions of fried alpaca meat. Afterward, we have coca leaf tea. Then Sebastian produces the large bag of coca leaves we bought in Cuzco. Spreading a cloth on the floor, he pours them into a heaping pile.

The ritual of sharing coca is perhaps the most symbolic act of *ayni* among Andeans. We sit around the pile of leaves and sift through them, selecting the most perfectly formed and greenest. I choose three leaves of equal size and put them together with two leaves in back and the other in the front to form a fan shape. I offer my *k'intu* to Sebastian. We take turns making and offering more *k'intus* by holding one between the first three fingers of each hand. The recipient accepts the leaves by taking them with both hands, thanks the giver, and performs the *phuku* before placing them in his or her mouth and chewing. The process is repeated and continues with people forming *k'intus* and offering coca to another until they are satiated, or until there are no more coca leaves left.

After the ritual coca sharing, they talk and joke for hours. Lorenzo tinkers with a battery-powered cassette player and, when he gets it working, plays folk music of the Andes called *Waynu.* It consists of a single vocalist, usually female, with a band composed of traditional Andean instruments including flutes. In modern times, the band sometimes includes an electronic keyboard that helps keep the beat in a polka style. The dance steps are a basic one-two side step. Couples hold hands, swinging them as they dance and sway with the music, circling first in one direction and then the other. Dancing in this manner induces a euphoric state, especially at high altitude after chewing mouthfuls of coca leaves.

Among the Q'ero, men dance together. Women dance separately or in a group with men. Rarely do couples dance together. Not being familiar with this aspect of their custom, I feel awkward and embarrassed when Lorenzo asks me to dance. He is a good instructor, however, and his enthusiasm is contagious. We launch into an evening of music and nonstop dancing.

The Q'ero are indefatigable and dance without a break. But I am impaired by the thin mountain air. After a few minutes, I feel light-headed and short of breath. Lorenzo is enjoying himself so much that there is no end to the number of songs he wants to dance to. Eventually, I excuse myself and sit down to catch my breath. The room spins and everyone is laughing.

No sooner have I rested, however, than Sebastian wants to dance with me. We dance several songs and then his older son dances with me. Then Lorenzo and his wife dance with me, followed by Lorenzo alone, and then Sebastian once again. This keeps on until they all have all danced and are satiated with music.

After the adults finish, the children dance. With the energy of fireballs, the girls move their arms like swings in a schoolyard. They whirl for hours, their joy boundless. If the batteries hadn't run out on the player, they would have danced until they collapsed.

We prepare for sleep. Including family members and guests, we are about 20 people and all the floor space in the hut is taken with reclining bodies. The children fall asleep immediately, while the adults settle into furs and wool blankets. I have my corner and snuggle into my sleeping bag on a bed of dry grass.

That night, I dream that two black pumas, a brother and sister, come down from the mountains. They peer at me from a rock ledge. Their yellowish-green eyes glow in the dark. They are heavily furred and their large paws pace rhythmically on the mountain ledge. They watch me for some time and then, as if called away by a voice only they can hear, they turn at the same time, leap, and are gone.

In the morning, I tell Sebastian about my dream. He listens carefully and then, as if thinking deeply, is silent for several minutes before he speaks. "To dream of a black puma is very powerful magic. To dream of two is awesome magic. It is a good sign for your journey."

After the hair-cutting ceremony, everyone dresses up. Sebastian (left), Lorenzo, author holding Yenika, Phillipa (Sebastian's wife), and Marcella (Lorenzo's wife), with children in the foreground.

Coca leaves spread on a handwoven cloth in preparation for communal coca chewing

Journey to the Mountain of Stars

It's early June 2004 and the moon is full. In the morning, before sunrise, it's still visible just above the peaks that form the west rim of the village. Lorenzo, up before dawn to fetch the horses, has returned with four. After a breakfast of potato soup, the Q'ero ready the horses and we prepare to leave Esparilla.

By midmorning, the moon has set, and the sun, higher in the sky, warms us. Rolando attempts to trim the mane of a speckled mare, but she bucks and has to be hobbled for him to complete the job. As Lorenzo and Guillermo finish packing the horses, Sebastian tells me that we are to journey for two days over terrain considerably more difficult and passes much higher than the ones on our entry. Our destination is the Mountain of Stars.

In Incan times, the Q'ero were one of three nations serving as custodians for three peaks close together in a crescent shape around a high valley. In the valley is a sacred stone, now covered over by a Catholic shrine housing an image of Christ called *El Señor de Qoyllur Rit'i* or in Spanish, *El Señor de la Estrella de la Nieve,* Christ of the Star of the Snow.

Legend has it that in 1780, while the Andean shepherd boy Marianito Mayta grazed his llamas in the area, Manuel, another boy his age, appeared. They became playmates. When Marianito told his parents about his friend, they were surprised, since no families lived in the area. So they reported it to the local officials who came to look for Manuel, but he disappeared into the snow, leaving behind a cross from the Tayanca tree. Marianito fell dead at the foot of the cross and, a short while later, an image of Christ was discovered on the sacred stone in the area the boys played.

Three mountains compose the setting for one of the most dramatic Andean festivals of the Incan year, *La Fiesta de Qoyllur Rit'i*, held at the end of May or first part of June. More than ten thousand pilgrims from all over the Andes gather in the small valley. Dancers dressed in colorful costumes whirl, while competing brass bands play nonstop music that goes on day and night for the entire four days.

The largest of the three mountains at 20,905 feet, Apu Ausangate is a perpetually snow-covered peak towering above the Andean plateau and the surrounding mountains. It is visible from Cuzco, but to get to its base takes six to eight hours, depending on road conditions, by bus. Nearby is the village of Mahuallane. The eight-kilometer uphill path to the other two mountains and the festival site starts here. Apu Sinakara is 17,950 feet high and Apu Q'olkepunku 18,116. Between them lies a lesser peak, Apu Qoyllur Rit'i, the Mountain of Stars. In Quechua, there are two words for star: *ch'aska* and *qoyllu*. The latter means "that which is resplendent, luminous." Specifically, *qoyllur* means Venus, the Morning Star. On the mountain is a glacier sacred from a time before the Incas and associated with fertility. As I understood the Q'ero, Apu Qoyllur Rit'i is a place in which heaven and Earth meet.

One way Sebastian and other Q'ero maintain their cultural identity is by making the journey to Qoyllur Rit'i every year at the end of the potato harvest. They do this partly to participate in the festivities that occur one week before the Catholic Feast

Day of Corpus Christi and last for four days, but mainly they come to honor *Inti, Pachamama,* the *Apus,* and their ancestors, and to see how far the glacier has retreated.

Incan prophecy has it that the next *pachakuteq* will occur when the glacier retreats to above 16,500 feet. This marks the time when *Inkari* will return to usher in a golden era. I am here with the Q'ero to participate in their ceremonies, undergo initiation, and witness the changes of the glacial ice. It has receded farther than at any time before, but, as I am to learn, it is still not above 16,500 feet.

Traditionally, the Q'ero arrive on the second day. They perform *despachos* on Apu Sinakara, and on the following day visit the shrine. On the fourth and last day, a group of special participants called *ukukus,* masked dancers representing mythical animals carrying long lighted candles, begin a procession in the cold morning darkness up to the face of the glacier. There they remove blocks of ice. In ancient times, these were tied on the backs of specially chosen *ukukus* who carried the ice the eight kilometers down the valley to the base of Apu Ausungate, and then on to Cuzco, a journey of several days. Now, only a few pieces of ice are allowed to be cut from the glacier, and these are transported by bus to Cuzco.

To the Incas, glacial ice represented frozen rain. Andean crops are watered by seasonal rain and the runoff from melting snow. In the equatorial sun, a bountiful harvest depends on adequate water. It was considered a good omen if the *ukukus* arrived in Cuzco before the ice blocks melted.

Upon arriving in Cuzco, dancers gather in the plaza of Saint Sebastian, a few blocks away from the Plaza de Armas, and carry the ice to the central cathedral as part of a raucous procession of Catholic and Andean imagery. The Incan ceremony, which occurred according to the phase of the winter full moon, has been replaced by the Catholic feast day of Corpus Christi, held immediately after the festivities at Qoyllur Rit'i. Statues of 14 saints, some canonized, but most specific to the Andes and unrecognized by Rome, are paraded down Marquez Mantas Street and then placed in the main cathedral on the Plaza de Armas. On the following day, the statues are paraded around the plaza. In Incan times, royal mummies were carried in a procession.

From the village, we set a moderate pace uphill toward the southeast between two bare peaks composed of a dark mineral ore. Black and white mountain caracaras, large hawklike carrion eaters the Q'ero call *alcachos,* soar from a high rock ledge and, flying just above our heads, float there for several minutes. They are close enough that I can see them turning their necks to get a better look at us.

This time, Sebastian's wife, Phillipa, accompanies us, along with their sons Vincente, Guillermo, and Rolando. Later, Jorge joins us with his wife, young son, and baby daughter wrapped papoose style with a tightly wound wool belt. Along the way, we are joined on our pilgrimage by a teenage girl and a young man with a white horse. Much later, Sebastian's 75-year-old aunt accompanies us.

We pass through a narrow space in the rocks and cross over a high ridge without difficulty. At the top, we pause but do not rest. A village made of exactly the same type of stone dwelling as in Q'ero is visible in the distance. We will not stop there, but continue on. Just before we reach the village, at the base of the mountain, we rest and water the horses. We are in a bowl-shaped high valley covered in short dry grass. Behind us are Apus Wayrumi and Willaqoya, peaks that form the northeastern border of Esparilla. In front of us, and to our left, the terrain drops off into an immense, desolate valley. In the distance are mountains shrouded in fog, and beyond them cloud forests.

The weather is in our favor and the day sunny and warm, but we are unlucky from the start. Just after leaving the village,

Sebastian's middle son, Guillermo, is thrown from his horse. He lands on spongy tufts of moss and is unhurt. Afterward, he appears ill, however; the usually strong 18-year-old is now pale and weary. More accidents are to occur. Phillipa is thrown from her horse and, later, a skittish horse steps on Jorge's ankle and injures it so severely that I fear a broken bone.

After a short rest, we continue on and, not far from the other village, we cross a sharp-edged ridge composed of loose rocks. The horses, generally accustomed to the rigors of the terrain, become nervous. Mine, a steady dark-haired gelding, is reluctant to continue. He prances sideways, twists, and threatens to rear up. Hoping to calm him, I dismount and photograph the village. As I adjust my camera, the clicking sounds make him even more nervous. When I attempt to remount, he bucks. I grip his flanks tightly with my thighs so as not to fall off, but the gelding turns with such force that I am tossed around on his back like a rag doll. I grasp his mane with one hand and tighten up on the rope that serves as a bridle with the other, but without a saddle, I slide around on his back violently while he struggles not to fall and I not to get thrown.

Though I am able to hold on, I feel a snapping in my lower back. At first, I ignore it. My immediate concern is staying on the horse and not being tossed over the precipice. He finally calms, and we make our way down the mountain and through the village; my lower back muscles tighten and I am in pain.

Once off the ridge, we pass through the village, in some ways more primitive than Esparilla. No one greets us. Even the usually curious children run and hide, disappearing into their stone huts or behind rocks.

We continue along a set of rolling hills. A trail cut into the side of the hill by repeated use over centuries provides the path and we snake along until we come to a wide plateau. Here we rest and the severity of my injury is apparent.

Dismounting is an ordeal. The pain is severe and requires

me to get one leg over the horse's back and then slide inch by inch on my belly until my feet touch the ground. My lower back feels like a dull knife is lodged in my spine and I have to lie down on the ground to get relief. When I try to stand, a stabbing pain buckles my legs as if they were made of paper and I nearly fall over.

After resting for a while, I manage to get myself erect and walk off some of the stiffness and pain. I'm encouraged. Perhaps it is only a muscle spasm. I mount the horse with difficulty, but riding makes the pain worse, so I go on foot. The plateau is at an altitude of 16,000 feet and the going is extremely difficult. My feet have healed well and though I am better acclimated to the altitude, at least enough not to experience further swelling, the increased elevation takes a toll. I am continuously short of breath and my energy diminishes by the moment. I struggle on in pain.

The plateau gives way to immense hills, and we continue along the side of one without cresting it. In the distance, an Incan road runs along the far side of a valley and then disappears to the northwest. Sebastian tells me it goes to an even more remote part of Q'ero before vanishing into the immense Madre de Dios jungle. Beyond that is the Brazilian Amazon. It is these rain forests that generate the clouds that shroud Q'ero much of the time.

It is another three hours before we arrive at Chuachua, Jorge's village. After circumnavigating the hills, we descend and walk into a narrow valley filled with boulders. A stream tumbles around them. I hear the sound of water against stone.

Jorge comes to greet us and helps with the horses. Despite my back pain, I am happy to see him and stand as straight as I can so as not to show weakness. He wears naturally dyed clothing the color of alpacas and the grass, and an orange and red *ch'ullu* under an Andean brown felt hat. As we exchange greetings, he points to a pair of condors gliding across the sky, first the male then the female following at a distance. The sun is already behind the surrounding hills and the air is cooling fast. A herd of about 50 llamas and alpacas group around the stone hut for protection in the oncoming night from attack by a puma or foxes. I find a flat spot among them and lie down on the grass to ease the discomfort in my lower back. The llamas adjust themselves to give me room and then settle down again. The odor of damp wool and the sweet smell of grass from their warm droppings are surprisingly comforting. Exhausted, I doze off.

When I awake and attempt to stand, the pain is crippling, and I have to lie down again before I fall over. It feels safe on the ground, but the sun is setting and the temperature is falling rapidly. It is much colder in Chuachua than in Esparilla. The air is cold, the ground becomes cold, the stones are cold, and the stream that runs through it is ice cold.

In a lifetime of travel to remote areas of the world, I have never sustained such an injury. The severity is out of proportion to the event that caused it, or at least that's how it seems to me. I calculate my choices. There is no way to get help if I am to need it. We are too far away. If help is available, walking in and out requires a week. I could rest for a few days until the inflammation subsides and continue on when I feel better; or I can wait until morning and, if improved, continue on if at all possible.

I am acquainted with the physical prowess of Indians and their ability to endure pain and I don't want to show weakness in front of them. I inform Sebastian that I need to rest for the evening and, if better in the morning, I will continue on with them as planned.

At first, Sebastian thinks I am suffering only from stiffness. Riding bareback with just a blanket as I had been doing is hard on the back and hip muscles. As a doctor, however, it is clear to me that I sustained a severe injury, possibly torn some spinal ligaments or, worse, ruptured a lumbar disc. Sebastian and Jorge confer and make plans. A cluster of accidents around the full moon makes them suspect the work of a *brujo,* an evildoer among shamans.

Not all shamans use their power for healing. Some, *achiq* in Quechua or *brujo* in Spanish, apply sorcery or black magic to control others or cause illness, accidents, unexpected bad luck, harm to animals, and even death. They often enrich themselves by selling their services to individuals who, motivated by greed or revenge, wish to harm another. Besides sorcery, the Q'ero believe that envy and jealousy are emotions strong enough to cause harm. Trickster nature spirits can also cause trouble like making travelers get lost in the mountains, but their mischief is less serious than that of a sorcerer.

While Jorge readies a palette of alpaca furs for me to lie on inside the hut, Sebastian prepares incense and herbs to treat my back. The pain is so severe now that I have to crawl on all fours, but it feels good to be out of the cold. The ventilation inside is so ineffective, however, that more smoke from the cooking fire stays inside than goes outside. It is so thick and acrid that I can hardly breathe. My eyes tear incessantly and my nose and throat burn. Thankfully, the smoke is less intense at ground level and, since my back pain is less when lying down, I stretch out in a corner.

The freezing mountain air gradually penetrates the hut and even with a down coat on, inside my sleeping bag, and on top of alpaca furs I am chilled. My body craves hot food, but the cooking process is slow. Finally, the meal is prepared and after a hearty meal of boiled potatoes and alpaca meat that I eat while lying on my side, I feel less cold.

When we finish eating, Sebastian discusses the situation with me.

"Is there someone envious or jealous of you? Is there someone who might wish you harm?"

I can't think of anyone in particular. My mind is confused due to the pain, however, and the altitude doesn't help as it causes mild delirium. Though I have many friends and few enemies, his question makes me paranoid, another symptom of altitude sickness, and I imagine several people who might harbor malicious intentions and who could be jealous.

"Perhaps," I answer.

"Since your pain came on so suddenly and is very strong, we suspect sorcery," he explains. "We will perform a ceremony to counter this."

Desperate for some relief, I accept their gestures and participate willingly.

Jorge prepares herbs and resins to make incense. After giving respect to the fire, he carefully takes coals from the fire pit and places them in a stone dish. He blows on the coals until they glow and then sprinkles resin over them. An aromatic smoke rises from the dish. It smells sweet and for a few moments refreshes the air in the hut, but it soon increases the level of smoke, making it even more difficult to breathe. Jorge holds the incense dish close and fans smoke over me with his palms. Sebastian stands behind him and chants imperceptibly. Then they fan smoke over themselves in the same manner, after which Jorge brings the incense dish to each person. We all need protection.

The cold increases as the night descends and, for the first time in the Andes, I feel vulnerable and worried. My right hip and lower back throb and I cannot sit up without pain, so I lie on my left side. The Q'ero huddle together for warmth and safety and whisper in the semidarkness.

Sebastian and Jorge spread coca leaves on a handwoven cloth. Jorge chews a large number of leaves into a wad and spits the mastication into his palms, on which Sebastian pours some rubbing alcohol. Then he rubs the mixture onto my lower back. It feels cold on my skin, and I flinch. Coca alkaloids have analgesic properties, so I am grateful for their attention and care, hopeful that the coca will reduce the pain.

They seem satisfied with their work and talk softly while the rest of us settle down to sleep. The boys cover themselves with saddle blankets and sleep in a row near the door. Jorge and his family lie in front of the fire. I am in a corner against the stone wall that leans inward at such an angle I am afraid it might fall over on us. Next to me are Sebastian and his wife, and next to her is the teenage girl.

Before turning in, Jorge has one last task to complete. In the light of a solitary candle, he reads the coca leaves to divine the days to come. After he spends almost an hour considering the implication of the leaves, I am worried that something is terribly wrong, but he concludes that all seems favorable and, pleased, disappears under alpaca furs with his wife and children.

"We leave at first light," Sebastian says from under the blankets. "The boys will go ahead by starlight to find a place for us to camp. We'll follow in the morning. Sleep now and rest your back."

Grateful for their help and kindness, I make myself as comfortable as possible and fall asleep. The coca leaf poultice seems to be working, as I sleep with little pain. At one in the morning, there is a bustle as the teenagers rouse themselves. Before they leave, they stake four horses for us in front of the hut. Taking two more, they ride into the night. It is quiet again, and I doze off, but find it difficult to breathe partly due to the pressure of high altitude on my heart and lungs while lying down and partly due to the lingering smoke from the fire. At three, the women get up and start a fire. It is hard to ignite dried alpaca dung and it takes at least an hour to get a blaze going, and until then the smoke gets worse. By five, hot food is passed around. We sit stiffly in the cold still wrapped in blankets and eat potato soup.

My back pain is considerably less, and after eating I can stand without assistance and go outside. It is dark and countless stars fill the Andean sky. Using a pole to lean on, I carefully walk around the hut to test my strength. Ice crystals crunch under my boots. Though I am in pain, it is much less and I can walk. The llamas, still bedded down, stir when I go by but don't get up. Even for them it is cold.

Jorge comes out and wants to know if I am well enough to travel. I tell him that I am confident I can manage. With that news, he packs the horses. Sebastian joins him, followed by the women and children. Though the temperature is much colder than in Esparilla, the Q'ero are dressed the same, in ponchos, *ch'ullus*, and sandals. They seem chilled and uncomfortable as they keep moving about and rubbing their hands together. I am freezing, even with several layers of clothing and a down jacket, wool gloves, and hiking boots.

Though my back pain is less, I am stiff and find it difficult to mount the horse. Sebastian helps me on the same gelding that I rode the day before, and we begin the final day of our journey to the Mountain of Stars. I have no idea that it will take nine hours over the most difficult terrain of my time in Q'ero.

In our group are Sebastian and his wife, Jorge and his wife along with his three-year-old son and baby girl of eight months, and the teenage girl from Esparilla. We make our way climbing steadily uphill out of Chuachua in the last darkness before dawn. The horses seem to know what lies ahead as they trudge forward, slowing their pace to accommodate the increasing elevation. Their breath comes in surges and with each exhalation they emit clouds of steam.

The early light of dawn reveals our path. In front lies yet another massive hill and beyond that another *suvida* or high pass. This hill seems to have no end. With the advancing morning light, the scenery becomes more spectacular than at any part of the journey. Large, weirdly shaped rocks are strewn across a landscape more lunar than terrestrial. Toward the top of the hill, a lone figure appears among the rocks.

Dressed in traditional Q'ero style with short tight black woolen pants, beige poncho, and *ch'ullu*—all colors of the Earth except for the bright red and yellow cap—he moves away from us without acknowledging our presence. Traditional Q'ero are known to wander the heights like alpacas or pumas, living off the land with the same kind of watchful, yet shy, intensity. As I watch, he vanishes into the rocks.

We walk on, deeper and deeper into the mountains. I feel as if I might never return to the world of noise and traffic and pollution. I wonder if we have regressed in time. Perhaps time stands still here.

The grade becomes increasingly steep, and the horses labor heavily with each step. Ice covers the ground where water oozes up from beneath the surface. The horses' hooves break through the ice, and it crackles in the cold air, so thin I feel as if I am not breathing at all. Even Sebastian and Jorge walk slower. No one speaks and the only sounds come from the snorting of the horses and their hooves on frozen ground. No one stops to rest or catch their breath and we push steadily upward.

The Q'ero are a rugged people. Conditioned from birth to endure the hardships of the high Andes, they can hike for hours at elevations over 14,000 feet, go without food or water, and need little rest. More amazing to me is that they have tremendous reserves of energy and can take off at a run like mountain goats when the need arises. They do this without getting winded, all the while carrying a load on their backs. Even the elderly are sturdy. Sebastian's aunt, for example, walks unassisted over passes of 18,000 feet. Children have the same ability. Jorge's two-year-old son, Everett, walks nearly the entire nine hours with the exception of the two highest passes when he rides with his mother.

Just before we crest the summit, we dismount and walk as is the custom to show respect to the *Apus*. Though the sun has yet to rise, the day is now bright and the sky cloudless. In the distance is a snow-covered peak.

"Apu Ausangate," Sebastian says reverently.

Astonished by its beauty and power, I fall to my knees.

Following Sebastian's example, I choose three perfect coca leaves to form a *k'intu* and perform the *phuku*. I bow and, touching my forehead to the Earth, pray to the *Apus*.

Fill my heart with love, so I express the beauty of munay.

Enlighten my mind with wisdom, so I understand the meaning of yachay.

Illuminate my way so that my actions come from a clear heart and mind, so that what I do is in the spirit of llank'ay.

Jorge searches for a low-growing herb. When he finds it, he selects several pieces of the plant and, holding them together with white quartz that covers the ground, he does a cleansing ritual. Passing the herbs and stone over my body, he utters incantations in Quechua to exorcise negative energy and keep away the bad spirits that may be following us. It is these spirits that they suspect are causing the accidents. Then Sebastian prays to the local *Awkikuna* and makes offerings of coca leaves to the *Apus*.

Once over this pass, we leave Q'ero territory behind. In the distance, the mountain drops before us to a sloping plateau. Beyond is a long, narrow valley bordered on both sides by steep hills. A river runs through it in smooth curls around boulders the size of houses. On the far bank is a village of six dwellings similar to those of Q'ero only considerably larger. At least a hundred llamas are corralled by rock fences surrounding the huts. At the end of the valley is a sheer mountain wall and above that more mountain peaks are visible. The snowfields of Ausangate loom over them all.

We begin the slow descent on foot, careful not to slip on the ice. The horses, pleased to be at lower elevation, meander randomly in front of us, cropping grass as they walk. When we come upon a spring, they break through the ice with their hooves and drink deeply of the cold water.

"*Munaycha,*" Sebastian comments.

Indeed, the presence of harmony and natural beauty is all around us. The sun, rising to the east, burns the surrounding peaks with gold. To our left, another snowcapped mountain comes into view. The Q'ero pause to honor the sacred mountain of their people, Apu Wamanlipa. As we watch, the sun rises over the surrounding hills and the snowfields turn golden in increments, then blue, and then a brilliant white.

"To become a *paqo,* you must know this *Apu,*" Jorge says.

"Do you have to spend time there?"

"Yes. Much time, many times, very high," he answers. "When you return, we will go there and perform another *karpay.* There are powerful places on Apu Wamanlipa. You will see and learn for yourself."

I understand what he means. To know the ways of a shaman, one must learn directly from nature. Through intimacy with nature in the wilderness, the shaman experiences life's mysteries. In this manner, over time, he becomes wise.

The message of the Q'ero, like North American Indians before them, is not only an ecospiritual one, but also one of continuous mysticism. This direct way of experiencing reality is not exclusive to Indians, but common to all mystical traditions. When one is thirsty, it is not enough to talk about water. One must go to the spring and drink. From the vantage point of these traditions, inspiration does not come solely from within a single individual, as with Western mysticism, or by transcending the self entirely as in Eastern forms, but in attunement with nature, the source of love, beauty, and wisdom.

We continue leisurely downhill to the valley floor. There we follow the river until we come to a well-traveled trail on the left bank. The horses trot along at a moderate pace, elated to be off the heights. It is not only the horses that feel lighter. Sebastian and Jorge jog behind under full loads. Depending on how sore my back is, I alternate between riding and walking.

At the end of the valley, the river empties into a larger, swifter one, and we cross over it on a narrow wooden bridge. On the other side is a small town. I'm surprised when Sebastian tells me they have a solar-powered telephone here, as nothing appears functional. In fact, the stores are empty and the school looks deserted. We pass through the town like riders in a Western movie going through a ghost town.

Just beyond the town, the Q'ero stop for the first rest of the morning. Although we've been traveling for five hours, no one appears tired. Still, the Indians spread their ponchos on the ground, and the women pass around freeze-dried alpaca meat called *churki* (where the Anglicized "beef jerky" comes from). Again, I notice that they drink no liquids.

After about 20 minutes, we continue along a well-defined trail through another, though much narrower, valley. It is warm and I remove my down coat and gloves. Sheep graze on lush grass, and Sebastian talks with the shepherds. The services of Q'ero shamans are highly valued in the Andes, and he is well known in these parts. We are on our way to Qoyllur Rit'i, he tells them, and he has no time now but promises to come again soon and tend to their needs.

Within an hour, we leave what fragments of civilization there were behind and once again begin to climb. The way to the next summit, Apu Akacuhua, is to prove the steepest and most challenging of the entire journey. The Q'ero focus on the task ahead.

At first the trail, as others before it, follows along a stream running through a picturesque valley. But this time, we are tightly hemmed in by steep rock walls as the valley narrows and we pass through a canyon. The trail rises steadily, as others before, and soon comes to an opening where we cross a grassy plateau. In front of us are immense snow-covered mountains.

We continue without rest under an intense midday sun. The Andean light is brilliant and the luminosity is, at times, stunning as if refracted by thousands of diamonds. The spaces between mountains and the valleys between seem inconsequential, making it difficult to judge how far away they are. Perhaps that is one reason the Q'ero don't give distances in kilometers or miles, but by the time it takes to walk from one objective to the next. Jorge tells me that we have four hours to go before we reach the summit.

Though the trail is well defined, as we gain in altitude the going becomes increasingly difficult. Knowing what lies ahead, the horses want to turn back and need to be constantly urged on. Phillipa's horse refuses to go farther and bucks her off. She is unhurt, or at least uncomplaining. Sebastian catches the horse and calms it enough for her to mount again.

Jorge leads the way on foot, followed by his wife, and behind her is Phillipa, both on horseback. Sebastian urges the other two horses from behind. I take up the rear, as I am the slowest. My back pain is still intense, but manageable, and I walk in silence leading the brown gelding.

We stop at a high alpine meadow to rest. From experience, I know that this means we are about to make the final ascent to the summit. The women take out boiled potatoes and dried alpaca meat, and we eat in silence under an azure sky.

After resting for a half-hour, Jorge and Sebastian adjust the loads on the horses. They add the bundles that they have been carrying, lashing them securely with handmade woolen rope. This way they can make the assault unhindered by extra weight. One horse, a rust-colored mare, tries to dislodge her load by rolling on the ground. Jorge runs toward her and pulls on the rope attached to the halter, but the horse rears and fights him. Hand over hand, he works his way closer along the rope until he is close enough to grab the halter. The horse will not be calmed and prances, agitated with his attempt to adjust the load, which has slipped to her side, and steps on Jorge's ankle.

Sebastian runs to help and takes over the unruly animal. Jorge limps back and I insist that he let me look at his ankle. It is already swollen with a large gash along his shin bone. He flinches in pain when I barely touch his ankle. I clean and dress the wound from my first aid kit and wrap his ankle with an elastic bandage. It may be fractured, and I advise him to ride the rest of the way. He thanks me, but ignores my advice. (To my surprise, in two more days, his ankle appears to have completely healed.) When Sebastian finishes with the horses, we resume the journey.

At the other end of the meadow, the trail narrows and soon disappears as we cross fields of rocks crumbled by eons of repeated freezing. The horses slow considerably as they labor to place one foot in front of the other. When they can barely move any farther, we dismount and walk behind them. We come upon a pristine lake, but continue on without rest until we arrive at the summit.

Though a glacial wind sweeps across the mountains, we pause. The view is majestic. At the top is a shrine of rocks piled high by those who have passed before us. Sebastian's wife selects a suitable stone from the ground and places it on the pile. To our left lies our final destination, the Mountain of Stars.

Jorge, limping, looks for white quartz. It is too high for plants to grow, so this time he uses only the quartz to perform another cleansing ritual. When he is finished, we proceed downhill along a llama trail and in an hour we arrive just above a valley surrounded by mountains. Thousands of people are already encamped in a basin at the foot of the glacier and along the rocky slopes rising from the valley. They have come here from all parts of the Andes for one of the most important festivals of the year, *Qoyllur Rit'i*.

The teenagers arrived before us and secured a camping place

in the ancestral area of the Q'ero on the hill above the west side of the valley. From this vantage point, we see the glacier, the peaks, and the trail into the basin thronged with pilgrims. The trail to Qoyllur Rit'i, in use since pre-Incan times, begins at the end of the valley to the south at the village of Mahuallane at the base of Apu Ausangate. To the north, at the end of the trail, is the Mountain of Stars; to the west is Apu Simakara; and to the east is Apu Q'olkepunku.

We arrive in the late afternoon. Sebastian and Jorge, with the help of the teenagers, move rocks to level the ground before spreading out blankets. The women look for dry grass and sticks to start a fire and, when it's going, begin boiling water for potato soup. They have no tents or other protection from the elements but camp under the sky.

The younger Q'ero are eager to take in the festivities. So after the campsite is suitable, Sebastian gives them permission to join the celebration. The adults stay in the encampment well above the valley and avoid the noise and confusion of the crowds below. Thirty to 40 thousand people attend the celebration, coming from as far as northern Argentina and Chile. The smoke from thousands of cooking fires is suspended in the valley like a cloud, and is so acrid that it is difficult to breathe and it burns my eyes. And even though we are a considerable way from the main activities, the noise of competing brass bands is deafening and continues for days and nights without end.

I am extremely uncomfortable the first night due to my injury and sleep poorly. I awake stiff and my back pain is worse. To make things more intolerable, the nights are unbearably cold, and I wake with my hair and eyebrows covered in frost. The Q'ero, wise to the ways of the mountains, wrap themselves in their ponchos and sleep with their heads covered in wool so as not to freeze their faces during the night.

My pain lessens as the day warms, however, and Sebastian

and I go down to explore the festivities. It is dusty and dirty, and the pathways are so crowded with people, horses, and llamas that it is almost impossible to walk. We stop in a tent serving as a restaurant and I order rice with meat and vegetables for Sebastian and fried trout for myself. Nourished with something more than the daily staple of potatoes for the last weeks, I feel stronger.

On the following day, my back is better and Sebastian, Jorge, and I climb Apu Sinakara. It is their custom to come here every year to perform ceremonies to honor the *Apus,* the snow-fields, and the glacier, which they believe is frozen rain. Its spirit fills the rivers and brings the rain that nourishes the crops and grass. In this way, energy is exchanged between humans and nature, which the Q'ero believe is the key to their survival.

Leaving the encampment in the morning in order to arrive by noon, we hike up the mountain until high enough that the clamor in the valley disappears, silent save for the sound of the wind among the rocks. Continuing higher, we soon are out of view of the festivities, and once again alone among the *Apus.*

When we come to a small lake, Sebastian selects a spot against a group of rocks and out of the wind. He begins in much the same way as in previous ceremonies, by selecting the most perfect coca leaves. Jorge helps by opening the little packets of paper that contain the offerings. Like them, I wear my Q'ero poncho and *ch'ullu.* This time Sebastian involves me in the preparations. I gather dried grass for the fire that follows the ceremony and help Jorge prepare the offerings.

Sebastian organizes the offerings, including a condor feather I have found along the way. Then, as I've seen many times before, he arranges each element with care to form a representation of the Andean cosmic vision.

With the *despacho* complete, Sebastian stands, holding the ceremonial bundle in both hands, raises it to the *Apus,* and prays. Then he blows into it nine times and passes it to Jorge.

He does the same, blowing into the bundle seven times. To my surprise, Sebastian passes the bundle to me.

"Hold it like this," he instructs. "Lift your arms upward and with a strong heart send your spirit into the offering."

I hold the ceremonial bundle in both hands as they have done, face east, and, raising it to the *Apus,* I send my voice on the Four Winds. I pray for healing of the hearts of men and for my own healing and the restoration of the Earth.

"Blow into it nine times," he says. "Now do it again, in the next direction, but blow seven times."

As I turn to the other two directions, he instructs me to blow into it five times and then pray again, followed by blowing three times until I have faced all four cardinal directions. When I finish, Sebastian takes the ceremonial bundle from me and places it on my head.

"You are one of us now and have the same responsibilities," he says. "Take this message back to your country. Pray to the *Apus* of your land. Do not forget us and we will never forget you."

The clouds part and the Andean sun pours down and warms us. This annual ritual, I know, is serious. Sebastian and Jorge consider it an absolute part of their survival as Q'ero. But this time is different. I am the first outsider to participate in this ceremony during *Qoyllur Rit'i,* and one of only a few to have been initiated directly by the Q'ero shamans.

I light the fire. The *despacho* bursts into flames and burns quickly. The smoke is fragrant, as Sebastian included different resins in the bundle, and it spirals upward and drifts toward the glacier.

Standing in the mountains with the Q'ero shamans, I finally understand. The oneness of creation is all around us. I sense it in the sky, the mountains, the snow, rocks, the glacier, the river below, and in my own heart.

A lone stone hut on the edges of Esparilla. *Apus* loom over and guard the pass leaving the village.

We approach the first pass on the way to the Mountain of Stars.

The women rest after the first pass.

Jorge's village, Chuachua

We approach the final pass. On the other side is the Mountain of Stars.

Author at the summit of the final pass

We approach Qoyllur Rit'i.

Dancers at Qoyllur Rit'i. The glacier is in the distance.

Ceremonial procession at Qoyllur Rit'i

Dancers in Cuzco on the Feast of Corpus Christi after the festivities at Qoyllur Rit'i

Ceremonial dancer

Ukukus carry blocks of ice from the glacier to the central cathedral in Cuzco.

Author performs the *phuku*, ritual blowing, on a
sacred bundle under the supervision of Sebastian.

Sebastian kneels and performs the *phuku* during the *despacho* on Apu Sinakara. Jorge looks on.

The Andean Codex

I arrive in Cuzco the following day after an eight-kilometer march down the mountain and a six-hour bus ride through dry valleys and over sepia hills. Apu Ausungate recedes into the background, appearing from time to time when the bus crests a rise. I feel that I am leaving something precious behind, and the closer to civilization I come the more nostalgic I feel.

The road is composed of dry clay and finely ground granite, and the bus kicks up dust so thick that even the slightest open window lets in clouds of talcum-fine powder that causes the passengers to gasp and cough. With the windows closed, the bus is stifling and unbearably hot compared to our days in the high mountains. Sebastian, who accompanies me, doesn't take off his poncho or *ch'ullu,* despite the heat.

The bus driver lets us off in Cuzco around nine o'clock at night. We take a taxi to Jackeline's house. My back injury is still troublesome and I find it difficult to climb the narrow, steep stairs to my second-floor room. The following days are warm, but the winter nights are freezing, which makes the stiffness and spasms worse. It's hard to sleep and in the morning it's difficult to get out of bed. I find it painful to walk or sit down. Sitting is the worst and, when I try to write, I can only sit for short periods of time before the pain drives me to lie down again. The cycle repeats. I feel better lying down but become uncomfortable and can't rest, and when I get up, the pain drives me back to bed.

Sebastian is concerned that my condition hasn't improved and he offers to make a poultice for my back. I'm curious about the ingredients, so accompany him, despite the pain, to the market. There we buy minerals, resins, and herbs from different shops, and a fresh cow's gallbladder filled with bile.

When we return, he grinds the minerals into powder in a stone mortar. Then he adds fresh herbs, a mixture of seven different types of sand, extract of arnica, and a white latex called *mato palo*. After these are ground and thoroughly mixed, he spoons out honey to make it sticky. Lastly, he puts in about two tablespoons of bile from the gallbladder we bought in the market and slowly heats the mixture on the stove until it becomes a sticky black paste. This he spreads on my back and waist, and covers it with newspaper. On top of that, he wraps a towel and then cinches the whole thing tightly with a belt.

He applies the same treatment nightly for several days. It helps somewhat, but his ministrations are not enough to eliminate the pain. This makes him suspect that sorcery is still the underlying cause of my slow recuperation. His suspicions are confirmed when we find that Julio, Jackeline's husband, a mountaineering guide, was thrown from a horse and broke his collarbone.

When Julio comes home from the hospital, Sebastian questions him. "Was there anything unusual about your accident? Were there any strangers near you?"

Julio tells us that he never rides horses when guiding a trip, but this trip was particularly difficult. On the return, he was tired and decided to ride since the horses were now free of their loads. The going was easy and the weather perfect. The horse, he told us, spooked without an obvious reason and, caught off guard, he was thrown onto his left arm and shoulder. The clavicle separated from his shoulder joint and splintered in the middle.

"Santiago," Sebastian says, "we must be watchful for malicious energy. This is not coincidence. Too many people in our circle have had accidents, and each involved horses."

He counts the injuries over the last five days: my back, Guillermo's fall, Phillipa's fall, Jorge's near-broken ankle, and Julio's broken collarbone. Five in all.

"What does it mean?" I ask.

"Potent sorcery is not easy to figure out," he answers.

To counter this, he insists we perform special ceremonies. "With the setting sun, you are to perform a ceremony to cleanse yourself and this house. Then, tomorrow at noon, I will conduct a *despacho*."

Skillful *brujos* are capable of disguising their mischief so they appear to be ordinary events, accidents that could happen to anyone. Envy and jealousy, if intense enough, can also cause harm, but it is not lasting and is easily reversed by a shaman's will or a simple ritual. Sorcery, on the other hand, has as its purpose the intention to create obstacles, distractions, disruption, harm, and injury.

I find the idea difficult to accept. So when Sebastian leaves for the market to buy incense and ritual objects, I spend the remainder of the day resting and thinking. If I accept the concepts, at least in principle, of a separate reality, synchronicity, luminous counterparts of plants and other natural things, and a shaman's ability to stimulate healing, why not believe in sorcery? I am not uncomfortable with paradox and am capable of holding different, opposing views of reality in my mind at the same time. Hate, jealousy, revenge, wishing the worst on someone who has done us real or imagined harm are part of the human condition. But psychic harm? This too, I was to see, is part of the Andean worldview.

When Sebastian returns, it is late afternoon. He instructs me in how to conduct the ceremony. "Use this *palo santo* for incense. Start it in the garden. Use your condor feathers, tobacco, and some *agua florida*."

Palo santo contains an aromatic resin and produces a sweet-smelling smoke. *Agua florida* is floral-scented water and is commonly used in Peru to attract good luck and dispel dark energy.

As the sun sets, the household gathers in the open court-yard. Jackeline, five months pregnant, is present and so is her 12-year-old son and young daughter. Her mother, suffering from bronchitis, is too ill to get out of bed, but we open the door to her room so she can hear. Julio sits on a small stool, his left arm and upper torso in a cast. Others gather as well, and Naomi, the servant girl, helps us invalids, flitting between Julio, Jackeline's mother, and me.

Under Sebastian's guidance, I light the *palo santo* and fan the incense with a condor feather. I light a *mapacho* cigarette and, as the smoke rises upward, I pray. As he has taught me, I summon the *Apus* and *Awkikuna* of the places from my journey. I ask for their help in removing any malign forces and request their protection for the future. Then going to each individual, I blow tobacco smoke over them while fanning them with the condor feather. I concentrate and, with my full intention, I will my consciousness and body to be free of all destructive energy. Afterward, I feel lighter. The others smile, talk among themselves; they too report feeling better. I sleep deeply that night without dreams.

At noon the following day, we go to a wooded area near Q'enco. Sebastian performs a double *despacho*. The first is like he has always done with elements of the three levels of existence, and he uses this one to perform cleansing rituals for Julio. But the other he makes purely for the *Apus*. It only contains elements of the upper world, *Hananpacha:* cotton, alpaca fat, large amounts of coca leaves—white upon green—and pieces of quartz.

Sebastian bundles both offerings together and, gathering Jackeline, Julio, their daughter Mikiela, and me, he summons every *Apu* around Cuzco and beyond. He calls to the *Apus* of California. His chanting in Quechua goes on longer than at any of the other *despachos* I've attended. His concentration is as intense as a puma's. I have not seen him like this before. Next he performs the *phuku.* When he is finished, he hands the bundles to me and I too perform the ritual blowing, but I am not blowing hard enough for him. He insists that I try harder. This time, I hold the bundles tightly and, facing east, I blow with all my heart. Then I repeat the process in each of the other three directions.

When finished, I gather dry grass to start a fire. Sebastian has selected a hollow in the rock and carefully arranges each stick of wood. A *brujo* can put out a ceremonial fire, preventing its completion and thwarting the attempts of the shaman to neutralize his sorcery. When confident the wood is right, he lights the fire and, kneeling before it, removes his cap and prays intensely as if willing it to burn. The dry wood pops with the heat and when every piece is on fire, he prays once more over the ceremonial bundles, orders me to place my hands on them and pray with him, and throws them on the fire.

We walk through a grove of eucalyptus trees toward the road to Cuzco. Sebastian follows us in silence. He does not let us out of his sight until bedtime.

The next morning is warm and sunny. Sebastian comes to my room early. *"Todo via duele?"* he asks in broken Spanish. "Still hurt?"

"Less," I reply. *"Menos."* I get out of bed and walk around the room for him to see that I am indeed healing.

He sits on the edge of my bed. At times, he informs me,

even these special rituals are not enough to dispel a powerful sorcerer's malicious intentions. In such cases, the master shaman must travel in his light body to find the sorcerer in his lair. Mortal combat may be waged. He implies that this is an extremely dangerous undertaking. Then he is silent, his thoughts turned inward.

In the following days, my back injury gradually improves. Julio's broken collarbone mends, and Jackeline's mother is cured and out of bed. With my recovery comes a greater respect for the challenges of the Andes and for the tremendous courage and endurance of the Q'ero.

In the mornings over breakfast, Sebastian and I talk of my work and purpose in Peru. He is concerned that the traditional Andean teachings are being misinterpreted by a growing New Age tourist trade. "The person with a clear heart and steady mind accepts his position in life and shoulders the responsibilities in front of him," he says. "Being a shaman is not about wearing beads and having long hair."

I know what he means. Andean Indians wear their hair short and pluck their facial hair. They are humble. Their teachings are Earth-based, practical, grounded, and are lived rather than preached.

I see that Sebastian has ambitions like everyone. But his are different. He is thinking how he will continue to feed and clothe his growing clan. If one or two children are educated outside of Q'ero, will they want to return? How can he preserve the traditions amidst increasing social and ecological pressures? If he raises a voice, will it be heard?

I feel that this comes with a lot of burden for him. He confides that in Cuzco he sometimes cannot sleep. He worries about his family in Esparilla. He thinks about the weather, the potato crop, and the llamas. There are times when he doesn't have enough money for food. No one goes hungry in his village. But Cuzco is different and he is on his own. He tells me that he may not eat for days, saving what money he has to buy supplies to take back to Q'ero. When I'm in Cuzco, I make sure he eats at least two meals a day. Nothing is ever left on his plate or mine, as he'll finish what I can't eat. Nothing is wasted.

"*Compadre* Santiago," he tells me. "You are beginning to learn our ways and understand the *Apus*. You already speak Spanish and are learning Quechua. You speak from your heart, like we do."

I don't know how to respond. I have been humbled by my back injury, awed by the mountains, and now his acknowledgment of my effort to understand the way of the Q'ero makes me feel strangely embarrassed.

In the evenings, we have long discussions with Jackeline and Julio about the needs of the Q'ero people and ways to help them. Jackeline's mother hovers nearby and translates difficult words from Quechua to Spanish, as neither speaks Quechua.

The subject of how to help is complex. For example, the Q'ero consider themselves an independent though not sovereign nation within Peru. They wish to continue to have geographical autonomy and to be able to guide their own political destiny. To accomplish this, they recognize the need for education, but the remoteness of their territory makes it nearly impossible for the government to maintain teachers. Alternate approaches have been tried. Maria Antonieta has taken Q'ero children into her home, raised them, and supervised their education. One young Q'ero, Sebastian's son Nicholas, graduated from high school in Lima. He aspires to attend university. The hope is that he will return permanently to Q'ero and teach. In this way, even in the face of ecological changes, the ways of the Q'ero and the Incan cosmic vision may survive.

Through these discussions, my years in Peru begin to make sense. Certainly, it is about fulfilling the Incan prophecy. One way to accomplish this is by helping the Q'ero and other Andean people achieve their own goals. But first, we must listen to them. My responsibility is to make sure that the White Brother's return, as in the Hopi and Mayan traditions, is a beneficial one. To realize that, I believe that I must live the Andean principles, as taught to me by the example of the Q'ero. Then these teachings, the Andean Codex, as I call it, can be transmitted to others, but only in a way that is authentic and has the approval of the Q'ero.

In essence, I've learned that there are five ethical principles that constitute the traditional Andean value system, which along with the Earth-based worldview of the Q'ero, forms an ecospiritual philosophy based on balance and harmony built on a deep abiding love that emanates naturally from an open heart.

To manifest such love, it is necessary to have a heart free of emotional pain and psychological distress. In addition, there can be no conflict between the heart and the mind. To a Westerner, this doesn't come easily. However, with patience, over time, if you practice the principles discussed in this book, little by little the heart is washed clean of the past. When you live in the present and listen with a clear heart, you are guided from within and can fulfill your destiny. It takes courage to live this way.

To review, the five principles are *munay, yachay, llank'ay, kawsay,* and *ayni. Munay* means to practice lovingkindness and live your life in beauty. *Yachay* means we need correct knowledge guided by wisdom to live in beauty. *Llank'ay* implies right action. Do good work and leave a legacy. Without making what you feel and think practical, nothing of lasting value is accomplished. *Kawsay* is respect for life and all life-sustaining processes. *Ayni* is reciprocity and the guiding principle of the Andean way. It means to give back, and to circulate energy, goods, knowledge, and labor for the benefit of family, society, and culture.

The Q'ero inclines towards integration and balance in all that the do, think, and feel. Their compass is beauty. For them, beauty and happiness are *yanatin,* an inseparable pair. Of the two, beauty, *munaycha,* is the more important as it is impersonal and can be shared, as when Sebastian pointed out to me lovely natural settings or when the day seemed perfect for ceremonial work. Happiness follows like a string attached to a balloon. When you hold on to it, you experience the joy of holding some thing that you know, by its very nature, will fly away if you let go.

Our tendency in the modern urban world, on the other hand, is towards fragmentation of body, mind, and spirit. We tend to either over work, acting out inner drives that are not based upon our own best interest or the good of the environment; over react emotionally, causing disruption in all that we do and for those close to us; or obsessively think about things to the exclusion of our feelings. Those who overwork, believing that only through excessive striving can we become successful and therefore happy, may accumulate material wealth, but find health and happiness elusive. When ruled by our emotions, we tend to over react without considering the consequences of our behavior. Harmony and peace comes when our feelings, thoughts, and actions are in balance.

The five ethical principles of the Andean teachings are important for everyone. The shaman, however, is held to higher standards. The shaman strives to maintain constant awareness while awake, in his dreams, and while journeying in his light body to other, separate realities. He is alert at all times to synchronicity, listens to messages from nature, and strives to create resonance between things, thoughts, and events. The shaman acknowledges the wholeness of being that is the Earth. He senses the entirety of the interconnected visible and invisible universe. His intention is like a clear mountain stream. The shaman's path is the way of light.

He has to overcome his own self-limiting ideas and be free of the opinions of others. When the rational, comparing, judgmental mind ceases its activity, an entirely different way of being manifests. One perceives through the heart. Then the heart and mind become one. Intelligence, once exclusive to the realm of mind, is channeled through the heart, the seat of higher consciousness; and the mind, free of the limitations of the physical universe, is now limitless. At this stage the shaman is a being of light, *Intikana*.

The master shaman is free of the fear of ego death. At this level, the shaman is a sage (*sabio* in Spanish), a "wise one." His presence is a benediction. In Quechua, such a one is called *Willaq Uma*, the "transcendental one," as clear as light.

In the Andean tradition, the voice of the enlightened sage is also that of the Earth. His every step is an act of respect and his thoughts are prayers. He is called *Amauta*, the "one of awakened consciousness," and a master teacher of the Andean worldview and code of life.

For me, to be an integrated person, without neurosis, at one with oneself, is miracle enough. In the end, the journey from becoming to being is just the natural state of all humans. By reconciling life's countless paradoxes, ambiguity is accepted as part of the grand scheme of things, and all things are in their rightful places. One is not tossed back and forth between emotional extremes. Achieving a state of harmony keeps one centered amidst daily events. One knows enough to get out of the rain as well as how to talk with crows and owls, listen to the clouds, and make peace with lightning. Enlightenment might not be the end at all, but the means to being a natural person.

Return to the Forest

After two months in the Andes with the Q'ero, I return to the upper Amazon. It is impossible for me to rationalize my ayahuasca experience further. I will learn no more unless I enter the stream of ayahuasca consciousness. Still, I'm apprehensive and, though no longer frightened at the prospect, feel anxious at the thought of facing the "mother" of self knowledge again.

Synchronicity is at play, however, and I have come to appreciate its resonance in my life so am not surprised when a Peruvian colleague in Iquitos, Elsa Rengifo, a researcher in medicinal plants, introduces me to a Shipibo ayahuasca shaman who is to assume an important role in the next stage of my ayahuasca training.

Mastering ayahuasca is not easy. It requires a lifetime of self-discipline, training under a master shaman, countless rituals and ceremonies, fasting and special minimalist diets of fish and bananas, sexual abstinence, and long periods of solitude in the rain forest. I have much to learn but feel my time in the Andes with the Q'ero has helped prepare me for this ancient path. I have come back to learn from the living forest.

As the Q'ero are considered the experts of Andean shaman-ism, the Shipibo are the masters in ayahuasca shamanism. A gentle and noble people with a great knowledge of healing plants, who consider themselves ancestors of the Incas, most Shipibo Indians live along the Ucayali River and its tributaries near Pucallpa, the capital of the Peruvian state of Ucayali, but some also live in and around Iquitos, five days downriver by boat.

Three days after our meeting, I am with a group of Shipibo Indians in the rain forest. The men are dressed in Western clothes: shorts or cotton pants, and T-shirts. The women wear more traditional attire: skirts embroidered with colorful geo-metric patterns and blue blouses with bright pink, orange, or yellow trim. Around their waists, they wear belts made of tiny white shell beads. Their straight black hair falls just longer than shoulder length and their bangs are cut square. Shy, but very polite, they keep their distance. Still, smiles flash easily and they are not afraid of direct eye contact. I feel comfortable with these people.

We walk through the forest to the ceremonial house. The *onanyanshobo* in Shipibo, or "house of healing," is set in the middle of a clearing near a stream. This is the traditional dwelling where Shipibo shamans work with the ill, conducting elaborate healing ceremonies that can last for weeks. Around us is the vast Amazon rain forest.

Ayahuasca is used to guide the shaman in diagnosing the cause of illness as well as in finding a cure. The shaman "sees" the illness as geometric designs. The spirits assist the shaman, especially hummingbird (*pino* in Shipibo) who writes a healing song with its beak. The "notes" appear as brilliantly colored geometric images, which the shaman sings. The "medicine" is the healing song. In this manner, any disharmonious energy pattern or collected psychic poison (*sano* in Shipibo) is trans-formed by the shaman's chant. Healing, for the Shipibo, is a return to harmony and beauty, *muy'so* in Shipibo. It sounds almost like *munay* in Quechua.

When we arrive, a younger shaman and several Shipibo women with a group of ever-present children await us. Teresa, a woman in her forties and the daughter of a shaman, heats the bark of *huito,* a tree containing a dark-blue, almost black dye used for ceremonial tattoos, until the sap runs from the wood, which she collects in a tin can. Taking off my shirt, I follow her instructions and lie face down on the floor on a cotton cloth she spreads out for me. She draws geometric designs resembling birds and animals on my upper arms, chest, and back. This process takes several hours. By late afternoon, the pigment is dry, and by sunset I am able to bathe in preparation for the nightlong ceremony.

The younger shaman has prepared a sweet-smelling herbal bath made from fresh plants he picked in the forest. Using a wooden ladle, I pour water mixed with pieces of leaves and flower petals over my naked, tattooed body. When dry, they dress me in handmade cotton clothes with geometric designs. Then we lie down on the plank floor to rest. As part of the preparations, we have not eaten or drunk anything since noon.

Long after sunset, when the forest is dark (I estimate the time to be about eight in the evening), the shamans bathe and dress in *chusmas,* the traditional long robes of the Shipibo. Each robe is covered with intricate traditional designs. They wear beaded headgear and a necklace made from shells and seeds from the forest, which makes a soft rattling sound as they walk.

The shamans proceed methodically and seriously. They softly whistle to call the spirits of the forest. This lets them know that we are going to drink ayahuasca and may enter the world of spirits, ancestors, and mythical beings. In Shipibo, ayahuasca is called *nishi* and the luminous presence of ayahuasca is called *Nishi Ibo.*

Then, they prepare *mapacho.* After much ritual blowing on

the tobacco, they smoke large hand-rolled cigars until they conclude that the ceremonial space is sufficiently cleansed. The Shipibo believe the ceremonial space should be sweet smelling, comfortable, and relaxing. They accomplish this with aromatic plants and tobacco smoke.

After the preparations and cleansing, we take ayahuasca. First the shamans drink and then I down the bitter brew. For awhile, the two shamans chat quietly in Shipibo while I meditate. The women make themselves comfortable on the floor or sleeping platforms. Most of the children are already asleep. It will be at least 20 minutes before the effects begin.

"When *la maración* [the local dialect for the Spanish word *mareo*, the dizziness] begins, stay calm. When it reaches its intensity, concentrate with all your force. Stay as if in the center of a storm and remain erect as a tree," the older shaman tells me.

As night approaches, the forest changes and large beige moths with gold-tipped wings appear. Giant fireflies light up in the clearing around the hut. The forest is coming alive. It resounds with an orchestra of insects and night-bird sounds. Rain starts to fall. The drops sound like distant drumming on the thatched roof.

At the first signs of the ayahuasca effects, both shamans bow their heads and concentrate. I brace myself for what is to come.

In another ten minutes, I feel dizzy. I concentrate as I've been instructed.

I hear a voice as if from the heart of the forest. "Welcome back."

Then the visions start. I see the ayahuasca as a luminous fluid in my stomach feeding the blue boa from my dreams. Awakened, it opens its mouth and drinks. Once nourished, it rises upward and out of my mouth. Waves of geometric designs in bright yellows appear. These give way to the same phosphorescent blue lines of my first session. A luminous web connects all things. When I open my eyes, the colors disappear, but apparitions appear.

A man stands behind the shamans. He's dressed in a *chusma* covered with very detailed geometric designs. Around his neck are many finely beaded ornaments. Later, they tell me this is the form the spirit *Nishi Ibo* takes and who stands behind a Shipibo shaman to protect the ceremonial space and guide his work.

Both shamans chant rhythmically for hours. Their simple songs are stunningly beautiful: "I am going to sing. Let's go together to cure the people," they chant. "I open the world of the perfume of plants to heal the people."

Periodically, they fan me with fresh basil and other herbs. I struggle to maintain consciousness by clinging to the sound of the songs. The sweet smell of the basil helps and I concentrate deeply. Within an hour, the colored visions fade and my consciousness soars out of my body and through the rain forest. I feel the power and immensity of the Amazon.

The shamans chant with astonishing alacrity, as one song follows another. "Clear away *sanos*. My songs are beautiful. They remove *sanos.*"

Sanos are seen as dark spots about the size of mosquitoes inside the ill person. If the singing is successful, they cluster and rise up toward the throat and are expelled through the mouth.

As the night deepens, the women join in the chanting. Teresa sings in a high falsetto voice that adds a level of beauty and grace to the ayahuasca ceremony, usually dominated by male shamans.

Then I see what looks like a mountain, bare of trees and grasses. The rock is covered in scales like that of a snake, but made of stone. There is a vertical fissure sliced in the face of the rock. As I look closer, I see that the fissure is actually a narrow corridor and at the end lies a double stone door carved in relief with intricate designs. Could this be the portal Sebastian alluded to?

The vision fades and the shamans and I chant until dawn. Of the women, Teresa is the only one who remains awake and sings with us. Before sunrise, we fall asleep on the floor. I awake several hours later feeling refreshed and vigorous. The others have gotten up before me.

Though all the vestiges of the visionary effects are gone, I experience a sense of attunement. I feel the immensity of the Amazon rain forest. Primordial. Ever new. Deep beyond comprehension. There is a pulsation coming from the leaves. It throbs like the beating of the heart.

Glossary of Quechua and Spanish Terms

Achiq (*Brujo* in Spanish): a sorcerer.

Agua florida: Spanish word for scented water used for purification and to keep away negative spirits during ceremonial work.

Aji (*Uchu* in Quechua): a chili pepper (*Capsicum baccatum*) native to Peru, though some say brought to Peru by the Spanish from the Caribbean, and extremely hot.

Akllas: divine virgins dedicated to *Inti*, the Sun, and cloistered in temples called Aklla Wasi.

Akulliy: to chew coca leaves.

Altomesayoq: Spanish-derived word signifying the higher level of Andean shaman-priests.

Amaru: serpent and symbol of wisdom.

Amaru kancha: temple of the serpents.

Amauta: a sage, wise one, one of awakened consciousness, a spiritual teacher.

Antisuyu: the eastern part of the Incan empire that extended into the Amazon.

Apu: tutelary spirit that resides in the high mountain peaks.

Aqha (*chicha* in Spanish): a fermented beverage made from sprouted corn and used as a staple in the Andes.

Awki: protective nature spirit that resides in caves, springs, trees, and rocks in the Andes.

Awkikuna: plural of *awki*. (Since there is no equivalent word in Spanish, the commonly used plural form is *los awkes.*)

Ayahuasca: the yellowish-brown, bitter tasting hallucinogenic drink made by slowly brewing pieces of the ayahausca vine (*Banisteriopsis caapi*) with chacruna leaves (*Psychotria viridis*).

Ayahuascera(o): a specialist in the use of ayahuasca for healing purposes, an ayahuasca shaman.

Ayni: the way of reciprocity central to Andean spiritual practice, and fifth principle of the Andean Codex.

Bruja(o): the Spanish word for witch or sorcerer.

Capac: one greater than a leader.

Capacunna: emperor.

Chaka: bridge.

Chicha: Spanish for the traditional Andean fermented drink (*aqha*) made from sprouted corn.

Chicha morada: a beverage made from Peruvian purple corn or *maiz morada* (*Zea mays* L., Poaceae).

Chinchaysuyu: the northern region of the Incan empire.

Choclo: an ear of corn.

Chuku: the hat with four pointed corners worn by Incan astronomer-priests.

Ch'aska: star.

Ch'ullu: the typical knitted colorful Andean cap with tassels hanging from the earflaps.

Ch'uñu: a thick, nutritious porridge.

Ch'uspa: small, rectangular, tightly woven bags used to carry coca leaves. (Fur bags made of baby alpaca, called *phukuchu*, are also used.)

Coca: the coca plant *(Erythroxylum coca)*.

Curandera(o): Spanish for healer.

Despacho: a ceremony demonstrating reciprocity for the purpose of maintaining harmony between the world of humans and spirits.

El susto: "soul loss" or a psychological condition characterized by withdrawn behavior, depression, and, when severe, loss of speech.

Faena: Spanish word for physical work. In the Andes, it is used for a communal work party.

Hanan: upper.

Hananpacha: the upper world of spiritual beings according to Andean cosmology.

Hanpi: medicine of the Incas.

Hanpiq: *curandero,* a healer.

Hatun: grand, majestic.

Huachuma: San Pedro cactus *(Trichocereus pachanoi,* or *Echinopsis pachanoi).*

Hucha: an offense, fault, transgression, or crime. When used in reference to sorcery, it may be thought of as malicious, heavy, dark, or malign energy.

Huito: a tree *(Genipa americana)* containing a dark blue dye used for ceremonial tattooing among the Shipibo Indians.

Inca or Inka: imperial ruler of Tawantinsuyu and considered the Child of the Sun.

Inkari: the title of the legendary Inca signaling the return of the rule of the Incas and the Golden Age of the Andes.

Inti: the physical sun and the spiritual presence inherent in the sun's life-giving energy.

Intikana: a being of light, limitless and at one with *Inti.*

Intiq churikuna: children of the Sun.

Kallpa: the life force.

Karpay: a grand *despacho* involving numerous shamans at which time initiations and titles may be conferred.

Kawsay: life, and fourth principle of the Andean Codex.

Kawsay pacha: the world of living energy.

Kaypacha: the middle dimension of Andean cosmology and the world of matter in which we live.

Killa: the moon.

Killarumiyoq: temple of the moon.

K'intu: three coca leaves symbolizing the three worlds of Andean cosmology, and the three ethical and moral principles of the Andean way.

Kuntisuyu: the western region of the Incan empire extending to the Pacific Ocean.

Kuntur: condor and totemic animal associated with the upper world and *Apus*.

Kuraq akullek: the highest level of Andean shamanic initiation.

Layqas: female sorcerors and healers.

Llank'ay: labor and the attitude of service to others rendered with love. The third principle of the Andean Codex.

Malo suerte: Spanish for "bad luck," implying that a spell has been cast by a malevolent spirit or witch.

Mamakilla: the moon spirit.

Mamakunas: abbesses of the Solar Virgins, *akllas*.

Manqo Qhapaq or Capac: the first Inka and founder of Tawantinsuyu.

Mapacho: Amazonian wild tobacco (*Nicotiana tabacum, N. rustica*) smoked in thick, hand-rolled cigarettes or in pipes.

Mate de coca: coca leaf tea.

Mayu: the Milky Way and a central aspect of Incan cosmology.

Milagros: Spanish for "miracles" but, especially referring to the heart-shaped medallions used in Latin America as offerings to saints or placed on religious relics as supplication for good fortune, healing, or the return of a loved one.

Moraya: a small bitter potato (*Solanum juzepczukii*) prepared by sun-drying and exposure to repeated overnight freezing until it becomes hardened. It is ground into flour used to make *ch'uñu*.

Munay: lovingkindness, the first principle of the five Andean ethical and moral code.

Munaycha (*Bonito* in Spanish): lovely, beautiful.

Naturales, los: Spanish for Indians still living in their natural state, naked and isolated in the forest.

Pacha: Earth and time simultaneously.

Pachacuti or Pachakuteq: the ninth Inca and the time between eras when the world is shaken and transformed.

Pachamama: the Earth Mother in space-time. In this book it is used interchangeably with Earth-time.

Pago: Spanish for payment to the nature spirits; however, in Andean manner, offerings are not payment based on fear of natural forces but more of a means of communication between humans and natural forces.

Palo santo: Spanish for "holy wood," a tree (*Burserea graveolens*) whose wood contains an aromatic resin which when burned produces a sweet-smelling smoke.

Pampamesayoq: a shaman-priest on the lower level of the Andean shamanic hierarchy who is a specialist in ritual sacred worship.

Paqo: an Andean shaman-priest.

Phuku: ritual blowing usually on coca leaves but can also be used for healing or directed toward the east as a symbolic act of offering the life force within one.

Pumarunas: Incan priests dedicated to ceremonies associated with the puma and important in festivals related to Cuzco, the city of the puma.

Q'ero: the indigenous people who are highly respected in the Andes for maintaining traditional customs and shamanic practices. (In Quechua, *qero* means a wooden cup but it is not the same spelling as the word for the Q'ero people.)

Qhaqya: the thunder spirit.

Qollasuyu: the southern region of the Incan empire that extended into Chile and Argentina.

Qorikancha: the Temple of the Sun in Cuzco.

Qosqo or Cuzco: the center of the Incan empire, the "navel of the world."

Qoyllu: resplendent, luminous as refers to stars.

Qoyllur: Venus, the morning star.

Quipu: an assemblage of cotton and alpaca threads woven and knotted that constituted an ancient Incan tactile system of mathematics and information transmission.

Quipucamayoqs: specialists in reading *quipus*.

Runasimi: Quechua, the language of the Incas.

Sach'a: the forest. In Amazonian legend a giant tree, *sach'a-mama* ("the mother of the forest"), is considered the master teacher of the mysteries of the forest.

Sami: calm, serene, beneficial, healing energy.

Saminchay: to wish someone good luck.

Samiyoq: one who receives *sami*.

Seq'e or ceque: the system of geographical lines radiating out of Cuzco containing at least 350 *wakas* (sacred sites).

Shacapa: fan made from the low-growing palm (*Pariana* sp.) used by Amazonian shamans as a rhythmical accompaniment to ritual chanting during ayahuasca ceremonies.

Soroche: altitude sickness.

Suyus: the four regions of the Incan empire.

Tawantinsuyu: the "four corners of the world" signifying the Incan empire.

Ukhupacha: the interior or lower world of Andean cosmology.

Uña de gato: the herb cat's claw (*Uncaria tomentosa*).

Unku: the pre-Hispanic black tunic still worn by traditional Andean Indians under their poncho.

Urin: lower.

Waka: a sacred natural setting or burial site.

Wakamayoq: a specialist in performing ritual offerings and tending *wakas*.

Watoq: a healer who diagnosed illnes through divination or in visions and dreams.

Wayruru: the red and black seeds from a tree (*Ormosia coccinea*) made into necklaces and bracelets used as love charms and protection against bad luck. Individual seeds are also used in ceremonies and given away for good luck. In Quechua, *wayruru* means "the most beautiful girl."

Willaq Uma: the fully integrated human being without neurotic tendencies and at one with the natural environment and spiritual worlds. A sage who could predict the future and cure illness with only his energy.

Willkamayoq: specialists in the ceremonial use of sacred objects.

Willkamayu or Vilcanota: the river that runs through the Sacred Valley of the Incas.

Wiraqocha: the world teacher and founder god of the Incas who manifests in physical form or in visionary states as a white-bearded older man dressed in a plain gray robe and holding a carved wooden staff. *Wiraqocha* in contemporary use is the formal address for a gentleman.

Yachay: the superior consciousness we arrive at through love and work, and second principle of the Andean Codex.

Yajé: another name for the ayahuasca brew.

Yakumama: immense mythical anaconda considered the ancestor or "mother" of the river-forest and all its creatures, and possessed of the power to heal and impart healing powers.

Yanantin: a divine pair of mountains or other natural formation, such as stones, sacred to the Incas. It is also used to refer to any pair of things that are synergistic, such as coca leaves and limestone.

Selected Bibliography

Ascher, M., and R. Ascher. *Mathematics of the Incas: Code of the Quipu.* Mineola, N.Y.: Dover, 1981.

Bolin, I. *Rituals of Respect.* Austin: University of Texas Press, 1998.

Calderón, E., R. Cowan, and D. Sharon. *Eduardo el Curandero: The Words of a Peruvian Healer.* Richmond, Calif.: North Atlantic Books, 1982.

Capra, F. *The Web of Life: A New Scientific Understanding of Living Systems.* New York: Doubleday, 1996.

Cieza de Leon, Pedro de. *The Discovery and Conquest of Peru.* Durham, N.C.: Duke University Press, 1998.

Clark, L. *The Rivers Ran East.* San Francisco, Calif.: Travelers' Tales, 2001.

Cobo, Bernabé. *Inca Religion and Customs.* Austin: University of Texas Press, 1990.

Davis, Wade. *One River: Explorations and Discoveries in the Amazonian Rain Forest.* New York: Simon & Schuster, 1996.

de Betanzos, J. *Narrative of the Incas.* Austin: University of Texas Press, 1996.

de Gamboa, P. S. *History of the Incas.* Mineola, N.Y.: Dover, 1999.

Ereira, A. *The Elder Brothers.* New York: Knopf, 1992.

Hemming, J. *The Conquest of the Incas.* New York: Harcourt Brace Jovanovich, 1970.

Ingerman, S. *Medicine for the Earth: How to Transform Personal and Environmental Toxins.* New York: Three Rivers Press, 2000.

Kolata, A. L. *The Tiwanaku: Portrait of an Andean Civilization.* Cambridge, Mass.: Blackwell, 1993.

———. *Valley of the Spirits: A Journey into the Lost Realm of the Aymara.* New York: Wiley, 1996.

MacLaine, S. *Dancing in the Light.* New York: Bantam, 1986.

Maturana, H., and F. Varela. *The Tree of Knowledge: The Biological Roots of Human Understanding.* Boston: Shambhala, 1998.

Mejia, K., and E. Rengifo. *Plantas Medicinales de Uso Popular en la Amazonia Peruana.* Lima: AECI, 1995.

Mortimer, W. G. *History of Coca: The Divine Plant of the Incas.* Honolulu, Hawaii: University of the Pacific, 2000.

Philip, Brother. *Secret of the Andes.* London: Neville Spearman, 1961.

Pina, A. V. *El Retorno de lo Sagrado.* Miguel Hidalgo, Mexico, D.F.: Editorial Grijalbo, 1990.

Ponce de León Paiva, Antón. *In Search of the Wise One: A Sacred Journey.* Woodside, Calif.: Blue Star Communications, 1996.

———. *El Anciano en el Lago Sagrado.* Buenos Aires: Deva's de Longseller, 2002.

Prescott, W. H. *The History of the Conquest of Peru.* New York: Rowman & Littlefield, 1843.

Redfield, J. *The Celestine Prophecy.* New York: Warner Books, 1997.

Sullivan, W. *The Secret of the Incas: Myth, Astronomy, and the War against Time.* New York: Crown, 1996.

Thomson, H. *The White Rock: An Exploration of the Inca Heartland.* New York: Peter Mayers, 2003.

Villoldo, Alberto. *Dance of the Four Winds: Secrets of the Inca Medicine Wheel.* Rochester, Vt.: Destiny Books, 1995.

———. *Island of the Sun: Mastering the Inca Medicine Wheel.* Rochester, Vt.: Destiny Books, 1995.

———. *Shaman, Healer, Sage.* New York: Harmony, 2000.

Wilcox, J. P. *Keepers of the Ancient Knowledge: The Mystical World of the Q'ero Indians of Peru.* Boston: Element Books, 1999.

About the Author

 J. E. Williams is a doctor of Oriental and naturopathic medicine. He is the author of two acclaimed medical books: *Viral Immunity* and *Prolonging Health*. His shamanic training and experiences with traditional Native Americans span a 35-year period, beginning in 1967 when he lived with the Yupik Eskimos of St. Lawrence Island in Alaska. He spends his time between Peru and Sarasota, Florida. For more information, visit www.andeancodex.com.

HAMPTON ROADS
PUBLISHING COMPANY, INC.

for the evolving human spirit

Thank you for reading *The Andean Codex*. Hampton Roads is proud to publish an extensive array of books on the topics discussed in *The Andean Codex*—topics such as shamanism, native wisdom, health, and more. Please take a look at the following selection or visit us anytime on the web: www.hrpub.com.

By J. E. Williams

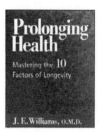

Prolonging Health
Mastering the 10 Factors of Longevity

Based on the latest medical findings, Dr. Williams presents a practical, 10-point plan to regain and sustain your health as you age by understanding and changing the ten major causes of aging. He shows how to strengthen your heart, revitalize your brain, rebalance your hormones, repair your DNA, and more.

Paperback • 464 pages • ISBN 1-57174-338-3 • $17.95

Viral Immunity
A 10-Step Plan to Enhance Your Immunity against Viral Disease Using Natural Medicines

This exceptional health resource sheds light on a host of emerging viral threats, from West Nile and hepatitis to Chronic Fatigue Syndrome and more, then calmly tells you exactly what you need to know and do to enhance your immunity and prevent, treat, and manage viral conditions.

Paperback • 496 pages • ISBN 1-57174-265-4 • $19.95

"Between *Viral Immunity* and *Prolonging Health*, all other health books are irrelevant, outdated, and inaccurate. Dr. Williams has set the new benchmark for rational medicine in the 21st century."
—Patrick Quillin, Ph.D., author of *Beating Cancer with Nutrition*

Shamanism

Traveling between the Worlds
Conversations with Contemporary Shamans
Hillary S. Webb

Webb invites you to eavesdrop on her conversations with 24 shamans—men and women who can, at will, enter into altered states of consciousness in order to acquire knowledge and healing power. For anyone who has ever had the desire to look at the world through the eyes of the shaman, *Traveling between the Worlds* is a treasure trove of insight and exploration into the teachings of this ancient path.

"A remarkable opportunity to 'sit with' modern teachers and healers walking the path of shamanism, and learn from them to awaken those same innate abilities within you."—Brooke Medicine Eagle

Paperback w/20 b & w photos • 272 pages • ISBN 1-57174-403-7 • $15.95

The Master of Lucid Dreams
Olga Kharitidi, M.D., author of *Entering the Circle*

At the invitation of an ancient secret brotherhood, psychiatrist Kharitidi travels to exotic Samarkand in the heart of Asia to undergo a profound shamanic healing. Her story reveals a different path to true healing that is available to us all.

Paperback • 240 pages • ISBN 1-57174-329-4 • $14.95

To Become a Human Being
The Message of Tadodaho
Chief Leon Shenandoah
Steve Wall

National Geographic photographer Steve Wall captures the images and words of Iroquois holy man Leon Shenandoah, who reminds us that our purpose in this life is to seek greater consciousness and a balance with Mother Earth.

Paperback w/22 b & w photos • 112 pages • ISBN 1-57174-341-3 • $16.95

www.hrpub.com · 1-800-766-8009

Traveling with Power
The Exploration and Development of Perception
Ken Eagle Feather

Beginning with his apprenticeship to nagual shaman don Juan Matus, Eagle Feather takes readers on a trip along the many winding paths of perception. You'll learn how to explore various modes of expanded consciousness using shamanism, lucid dreaming, out-of-body experiences, and more.

Paperback • 280 pages • ISBN 1-878901-28-1 • $12.95

Tracking Freedom
A Guide for Personal Evolution
Ken Eagle Feather

Building upon the teachings of Toltec seer don Juan Matus, *Tracking Freedom* shows you how to read auras and other energy fields, balance chakra energies for personal growth, and find and travel a path with heart.

Paperback • 280 pages • ISBN 1-57174-093-7 • $13.95

Spirit Animals and the Wheel of Life
Earth-Centered Practices for Daily Living
Hal Zina Bennett

In this technology-mad world, we are increasingly losing our connection to the natural world. Bennett offers an accessible form of eco-spirituality in which personal power animals—including the eagle, badger, wolf, bear, mountain lion, and mole—are the guides and teachers, and shamanism is the means by which we work with them.

Paperback w/illustrations • 192 pages • ISBN 1-57174-216-6 • $13.95

www.hrpub.com · 1-800-766-8009

Spiritual Practices

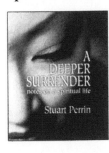

A Deeper Surrender
Notes on a Spiritual Life
Stuart Perrin

A unique blend of Eastern mysticism with Western sensibility, *A Deeper Surrender* is an indispensable guidebook to the often rugged terrain of the soul. Stuart Perrin is an experienced teacher who's "been there," and can help you through the darkest valleys of your spiritual quest.

Paperback • 256 pages • ISBN 1-57174-217-4 • $14.95

The Way Back to Paradise
Restoring the Balance between Magic and Reason
Joseph M. Felser, Ph.D.

Our culture denies peak mystical experiences, yet this mentality only weakens us by cutting off the creative and magical half of ourselves. In this absorbing book, Felser centers his argument around a richly imagined reinterpretation of the biblical story of Eve, and shows that it is precisely these peak experiences that allow us to unleash our creative potential and transform our lives.

Paperback • 264 pages • ISBN 1-57174-380-4 • $14.95

Muddy Tracks
Exploring an Unsuspected Reality
Frank DeMarco

Foreword by Colin Wilson

Muddy Tracks shows by personal example how inner guidance, astral travel, dream analysis, past-life recall and other techniques can help you to develop your psychic gifts, and, more importantly, discover the hidden spiritual substance of your life.

Paperback • 328 pages • ISBN 1-57174-362-6 • $15.95
Also available in hardcover: • ISBN 1-57174-257-3 • $21.95

www.hrpub.com · 1-800-766-8009